KNOW THYSELF

A workbook and journal for modern living

Introduction

Do you ever feel success is always just around the corner, but the corner is never reached?

Or that you are not quite ready for happiness and that dissatisfaction gnaws at your gut?

What about money? There is never really enough, is there?

You drift along in life, not quite making it.

And what about God? You believe there is a creator – after all, something created all of this, yet he, she, it does not seem to be there for you.

If you have the *will* and the *desire*, Know ThySelf will show you that your life can work and that you are not alone.

It will teach you to identify and clear the issues that are blocking you. It will also teach you that when you remove your fear you will see that you are a child of God and will know its support.

Know ThySelf is a workbook that you work through at your own pace. There are many lessons, and each lesson makes use of contemplations. These can take you to aspects of yourself that you didn't know existed. All your revelations are journalised so you can plot your growth as you go along.

Know ThySelf, a Workbook for Modern Living

GRAYSONIAN PRESS
Inspirational books that change the world

Published by Graysonian Press www.graysonian.com pat@graysonian.com
+ 0836101113 (South Africa) 0450260348 (Australia)

Copyright © 2009 Pat Grayson

Printed in Australia 2013
First printed in South Africa

All rights reserved under international copyright conventions. No part of this book may be reproduced, stored in a retrieval system, or transmitted in any form or by any means electronic, mechanical, photocopying, recorded or otherwise without written permission from Graysonian Press.

Whilst every care has been taken to check the accuracy of the information in this book, the publisher cannot be held responsible for any errors, omissions or originality.

Many quotations are used. Where the source is known, they are acknowledged. For those that have not been acknowledged, our humble apologies. If you inform us, we shall rectify this in the next print version.

Dedication

If it was not for Denise, this book would not have been written.

Mum, your influence on me cannot be measured. You are the sun that I revolve around.

I thank my guides and angels, known and unknown, for their support in my personal growth.

My appreciation goes out to those people who hurt me and to those I hurt. Thank you for the lessons.

To Judy Barnes – a friend who taught me so much about writing.

Journey of Self (overcoming fear)

It seemed that I was born into darkness, where images could just be discerned. Roots of trees as thick as a man's body lay strewn above the ground, like slumbering serpents supporting trunks of massive height and girth. Thick humus carpeted the ground, debris from the solid canopy that hid the sky far above. It was soft to walk on, damp and mildewy. The grotto of my mind was a cold and thriving place for all manner of creepy-crawly things, things that slithered in the near dark. Leaves constantly rustled as some creature scurried away from a predator, or was the predator. Things growled and hissed as combatants struggled for survival.

In this cauldron of my early life, fear clutched at my gut and was a constant companion. Somehow, some way, I knew that to stay in this claustrophobic dungeon was to be vulnerable. I had endured this tomb of mind from childhood to adulthood. But a sense niggled at my mind, pushing me to move and seek something better. I did not know where this sense came from, but I felt it could be trusted. I determined to leave the relative security of the known for the unknown, and set off to find myself.

At first my progress was slow, and for a time it seemed to get even darker, which scared me more. But as I grew and developed, I learnt that to move from one mind space to another can incur darkness, as our fear takes over. I continued the journey, stumbling on, falling over life's impediments and overcoming difficulties. For this journey of self I was alone. I had to be, as no one could share it with me. Nor did I have any idea of the direction to take – how could I? I did not know the destination and if I did, how could I know if I had made it? Never having faced myself before, it felt awkward, like wearing a coat backwards.

It was difficult cutting through the thick bush that clung to me, a thousand silent arms – arms like beggars searching, restraining and clutching, demanding. The terrain was always uphill. My arms and legs were exhausted from the pushing and pulling as I climbed higher and higher. At times I would slip and plummet to a point where I had been some time before. I would lie there feeling sorry for myself and wonder what lesson I was supposed to learn. It crossed my mind many times to give up, as the journey was too arduous. Nevertheless, I struggled on.

After a while I started to learn the ways of my inner realm and it became easier. I developed an assurance that things would keep improving and so I was able to cover more ground. The once formidable dark and dank depths of my inner self did not seem so hostile. It was the same, yet different. What had changed? I had, and as if to support my evolution, I was given beams of light that radiated through the bush, showing the way. It illuminated the jungle of my mind, giving beauty and form to its interior. But there was more journeying to be done, and so onwards and upwards I clambered.

Once I came face to face with glowing eyes, from a menacing long black shape. It snarled and spat, while its breath soured my nostrils. Had this creature confronted me in the past, it would have devoured me, but I held my nerve and it slunk away.

Although it seemed to be years that I had been on this journey, I sensed that I was making progress, as the darkness gradually gave way to light. High above, through the trees, was blue. I could not understand what this was, but felt it to be friendly. As I continued, somehow I knew that my direction was correct and that each step took me assuredly to a warmer place.

Suddenly, I was out of the jungle and on a stone ledge that jutted out of the valley wall. The sun shone a golden protection, nurturing and comforting. The open space was liberating.

I looked over the jungle that had previously owned me and could see the rivers that I had forded and the scrub that had cut my hands. At the time I could not see any logic or plan to it, but now it was all so obvious and perfect. From my position of elevation, the wilds were beautiful. Yet to reach this point I had been obliged to travel through those wilds and endure the experiences.

I am now stronger, forged in the knowledge of who I am, but I also know that the journey of self is never over; there will be new internal frontiers to conquer. But for now I revel in the joy of knowing that I have won the victory of the journey of self.

TABLE OF CONTENTS

The Course (Know ThySelf - KTS)	8
The premise of this book	8
What most people want from life	11
Why knowing Thyself is so important	11
How to get the most from this book	13
Spirituality	15
Introspections and preparation	17
Tools for processing	24
Life's lessons	26
Life's purpose	51
Attitude	67
Ego	73
Your journal	81
Acceptance	84
Love or fear	90
Taking Responsibility	95
Self Esteem	104
Confidence	106
The power of choice	115
Fate	124
Success	127
Failure	134
Affirmations and visualisations	146
Abundance	150
Forgiving	151
Guilt	162
Courage	165
Family	167
Generosity	171
Financial affairs	174
Goal setting	182
Happiness	186
Health	192
Love	193
Moral code	207
Creating your own reality	211
Luck	214
Stress`	218
Patience	221
Freedom	222
At the end of your life	225
End notes	228
Introspections – in greater detail	230
Reference	238

THE COURSE (Know ThySelf - KTS)
KTS is a ten-week course consisting of daily lessons and introspections.

Each day's lessons will take approximately forty minutes. It does not matter if you miss out a day here and there, but it would be best to set a goal to do at least five lessons per week. Speeding up will not make you learn or grow any faster. Take your time and progress in a consistent and thorough way.

There is absolutely no doubt that if you dedicate yourself to the lessons and make this work a part of your life, you will grow beyond your wildest dreams. It may not always be easy. Sometimes growth will be difficult and challenging but remember you can't grow a healthy crop without lovingly clearing the land and planting the seeds. By investing the time, your work will produce a rich and rewarding harvest.

Unlike most courses, KTS is experiential, not intellectual. In this course you will need to roll up your sleeves and get your hands dirty. Most psychologists will agree that to transform, you have to dig deep.

Your first journal entry
You will be doing a lot of journal entries over the course. Are you prepared to roll up your sleeves and work hard to improve yourself?
....
....
....
....
....
....

Knowing others is wisdom: knowing the self is enlightenment.
— Tao Te Ching

The intuitive mind is a sacred gift and the rational mind is a faithful servant. We have created a society that honours the servant.
— Albert Einstein

THE PREMISE OF THIS BOOK
I believe that the purpose of life is to have an ongoing relationship with God. That is, to become one with The Source. However, we invariably have 'issues' and get so lost in them that we get distracted from our natural path. For instance, it would be difficult to feel the Supreme Being's love if your husband has just beaten you up for

the umpteenth time or if you are always in and out of jobs, continually in debt and stressed out about a lack of income. Understandably your focus would be elsewhere – your issues are impediments.

God awakens us through dysfunction. We have a choice to wallow in our issues or to resolve them. By resolving them we open the way for growth towards our higher self and God.

How do we resolve them? By becoming aware of our disruptive life patterns and getting to know ourselves. Then and only then can we resolve these issues.

This workbook will help you identify your issues and give you tools to clear them.

Your first journal entry: are you happy with your life?
....
....
....
....

Peace
This course will teach you how to be at peace with yourself and your environment. What do I mean by peace? It's a life that does not operate with a frantic mindset. Without peace there can be no connection to God.

Are you at peace with yourself and your life?
....
....
....
....

If you were to die today, would you be satisfied that you had achieved all that you wanted to achieve?
....
....
....
....
....
....
....

....
....

Do you know who you want to be, and are you that person?

....
....
....
....
....
....
....

THE BIG 5

I am about to teach you The Big 5. The Big 5 will help you for the rest of your life, if you allow it to. The sooner you learn to put The Big 5 to work for you, the better your life will be. These 5 disciplines are a mixture of self help, being positive and spirituality. They are:

1) Look within to remove all self esteem issues, fear and negativity.

2) Believe that you are capable of achieving what you set out to achieve.

3) Generate your visions. If you can't see it, then it is not likely to happen. Generate visions of good happenings.

4) Take action towards your goals as God helps those who help themselves. Sitting and waiting will not bring results.

5) Lastly, create a relationship with God. God is the glue that holds all the above together. God is the grease that lubricates the above.

Are you willing to invoke The Big 5? ....
....
....
....
....

Gnosis - **to know the divine spark by direct experience.** This is different from trust and faith.

WHAT MOST PEOPLE WANT FROM LIFE

The following three responses to the question "What do you want to get out of this course?" are typical of those from people who have attended the KTS course:

1) To live a happier life and investigate the existence of God.
2) I want to be close to God, be happy and know that everything is possible.
3) I want to surrender my life to my higher power so I can fulfil the highest purpose that I'm here to fulfil.

The above three responses represent what most participants want, that is, to find their creator and to be happy.

What do you think of the above three points and do you have any to add? ....

....
....
....
....
....

WHY KNOWING THYSELF IS SO IMPORTANT

We cannot become what we need to be, remaining what we are. -
Unknown

If you do what you've always done, you'll get what you've always got.
– Unknown

Knowledge + (Applied) Wisdom = Peace or Knowledge of Self = Empowerment

You are bombarded with thoughts every second of every day. Most steal your clarity and unconsciously mould you into a form that you do not like or perhaps are not even aware of. They rob you of your innate power and control your life. Negative or unconscious thoughts make you do and say things that are not compatible with who you are or who you want to be.

If you knew how many thoughts direct your life you would be stunned. In just one year there can be millions and each and every one of them has the power to reduce your focus and stifle your potential or to assist you in manifesting what you want. Most thoughts however are of a revolving theme, themes that revolve thousands of times, thereby creating your circumstances. These can be emotive issues, frustrations, impatience, anger, peevishness and defensiveness, all taking you down the wrong route.

The things that you tell yourself are the things that you become. So does it not make sense to become aware of what you think?

Because of the nature of our society, where everyone else around us appears to be enduring some form of negative thinking, we don't see it and all seems normal. Initially, to rectify our habitual thinking takes courage and persistence. We begin by bringing the thoughts that consume our interior into our awareness, the thoughts that in the past have built the patterns that set our life. When we slow down our logical brain, we can see clearly where our direction is contrary to what is good for us - where we are out of alignment with what we truly want.

To know yourself is to understand the areas in which you are strong and to acknowledge your weaknesses. From that point of self-disclosure, you can begin to make miraculous changes.

Your Life's Work

The purpose of this workbook is to give you methods and tools to assist you to process as many aspects of your life as possible. It covers many topics and these will have a different significance at different stages of your growth. It is a working companion that will inspire you on a daily basis. You live in a limited and restricted reality. But by understanding yourself, you can remove some of the restrictions.

To know thyself is a wonderful and unique journey of self-discovery. At times this may feel like a daunting task but you will reap the benefits of untold rewards. The path may be long and you are likely to encounter many twists and turns along the way. You will soon realise that the journey is limitless and has no real end. Each key you receive along the way will unlock another door. Good luck in your internal travels. Remember – **The Kingdom of Heaven lies within you.**

Cognitive

You must take responsibility for your own development. Therefore you need to be conscious as the therapy is cognitive therapy. It is only through being cognitive that it can be effective.

HOW TO GET THE MOST FROM THIS BOOK

This book is not a quick fix. It is an interactive manual. I suggest that you work through this **work**book more than once. Each time you go through the process you will derive further benefit. At first, some of the sections may seem irrelevant but as you grow and develop and re-read it, the essence of the lessons will seep in and become more integrated into how you live your life on a day-to-day basis.

Did you notice the word **work** in 'workbook' was emphasised?

As you proceed through KTS you will see many **Stop points** (in rectangular boxes). Each is an issue pertinent to that topic. Take the time to work through these and think about how they apply to you.

There are many INTROSPECTIONS (introspection and introspect are my words). These appear on an ad hoc basis and are given to you to allow you to focus in greater detail on the issue that requires clarity. This book proposes that you analyse the many facets of your life. Over time, you are advised to introspect on as wide a range of issues as possible. As you progress you are offered a list of possible topics for self-analysis.

As a writer I use stories to teach. I call these 'the ramblings of a writer'.

Lastly, you will derive greater benefit if you write down and record your thoughts, lessons and anything that annoys or resonates with you in the journal in the space provided.

Willingness

This book or any other book on self-help will only work for you if you are driven by an outcome and have the will to succeed.

Let me give you an example. John and Peter are runners. They are of similar abilities and builds. John has won many races and has aspirations of becoming an Olympic champion. Peter runs because girls run and Peter likes girls. He couldn't care less about winning races because to do so requires hard work. He is not willing to sweat, strain or hurt himself - 'No way,' he thinks.

John is a champion in the making and is willing to put in the hard work. Peter is not a champion in an athletic sense but he does know lots of girls. He's willing to do anything, even run to meet a new lady.

Both of the above men have a will to achieve a given goal. Do YOU have the will to help and heal yourself?

The opposite of will is apathy. Without the will you achieve nothing.

Your design is to achieve and you can achieve far more than you could ever imagine. But you must have the will. Think for a minute of a person who has been saying for years that s/he will create something better. But it doesn't happen as s/he is too apathetic to go and do it. That person may be you.

Self Help = Improving your life

Have you ever asked what self-help really means? Stating the obvious, it means helping yourself. You do this with the aid of this and other books, videos, etc, all of which could be called tools. Continuing from the willingness above, these tools can only help if you have the will to apply them.

Here is a poem that I wrote, called Express Itself...
Compare your life to that of a tree -
At first there is a seed.
You a foetus
The tree germinates
You are born
Strong green shoots search for sunlight
You reached for mother's breast and experiences
The sapling gets stronger, firmly burying roots into nurturing soil
Whilst you walk, speak and start to express individuality.
Years pass, the tree has grown and although not of full height
Does not blow or wash away
You have grown to fend for yourself; life is spread before you
But wait a minute, what happens next, the tree can remain in shadow
Short of sunlight
It has a choice - remain stunted or express itself!
You have the same choice - grow or remain unfulfilled
It is in the tree genes to shrug off inadequacy
To grow strong, tall and ever upwards
To arch the sky and take its place in the sun.
What about you, can you fulfil your natural right and shrug off imperfection?
or do you languish under the shade of others, stunted and withered?

Remember if you were already perfect, you would not be here.

Journal notes: ....
....
....
....
....

SPIRITUALITY = *The essence of what we are*

Many people think that by embracing a spiritual life, they can ignore their human issues. On the contrary, we cannot efficiently embrace The Divine if our human failings are not attended to. By not clearing 'your' issues you actually block your spirituality. You need to understand that the mind, especially a negative mind, blocks the soul from emerging.

I am going to pause here for a minute to say that throughout this work I call that 'Mysterious Power' the Supreme Being, as well as other names. I suggest that you use a name that is comfortable for you, such as God or Allah, etc. You may not believe my premise, but I ask you to continue reading and to *keep an open mind* while you work with the processes. After all, what have you got to lose?

The following is loosely based on writings by Gopi Krishna
There is intelligence in animal migration, cell division and biology, as there is in all nature.
There would be no intelligence in us if there were no intelligence behind the universe.
It is the intelligence behind the universe that I refer to as God. I have a reverence for that intelligence.

Throughout this work I suggest that, if your life is to work, then it is more likely to come about if you have a spiritual belief. My life did not work until I started to find The Divine within me. I shall use the sea as an analogy.

There is the sea which pulsates with life and energy. I am part of the sea and yet I cannot see it, nor can I comprehend its vastness. I say to myself what is the sea? I am made in its likeness but I don't understand it.

For the first part of my life I was separate from the sea, I was a drop (perhaps a drip is a better way of putting it). As a drop I was not able to flow with the energy of the currents. I was out of sync with the tides. I did not know the grandness of the seaweed, nor the coral. I did not comprehend its magnificence. Yet as a drop, I thought that I knew it all and that I was ok. For years I swam around in my own little ocean to no avail. I swam harder and still got nowhere. Still my little drop was on its own and drying out.

It was only when I started to understand how we as humans work and how the Universe works that I found myself back as a comprehensive component of the sea. Only when I aligned myself with The Creator (who obviously is the sea in this analogy) did I truly start to connect with the Universe and to master myself and life. We are one, but as a drop I separated my self from the whole.

Another analogy: If the strings of a guitar are too loose, there will be sound but not great sound. If the strings are too tight, the sound will also be discordant. To give the best sound the strings have to be finely tuned to offer the correct vibration. They need the right balance, neither too tight nor too loose. As humans we also have to have the right vibration. We can only achieve the right vibration when we align ourselves with The Divine. If our vibrations are too fast we will survive, but the tune of our life will be of poor quality. If you are in balance with the Universe, your life will work.

God is at home, it is we who have gone for a walk.
— Meister Eckhart

Without divine assistance I cannot succeed; with it I cannot fail.
— Unknown

In whatever way a human being shall seek me, in that way he can find me. The paths are many, but ultimately all come to me.
— Bhagavad Gita

You are not here to contact your higher self: you are here to claim it.
— Unknown

What is God to you? ....
....
....
....
....

'And have we now forgotten that powerful Friend? Or do we imagine we no longer need its assistance? I have lived... a long time; and the longer I live, the more convincing Proofs I see of this Truth, that <u>God</u> governs in the Affairs of Men.'
— Benjamin Franklin

Mind, body and spirit

As humans we have three main components. These are mind, body and soul. A lot of people think that they can bypass the responsibility of the mind and head straight towards their spiritual view. Every aspect of our being needs to be holistically integrated. One does not work without the other.
For instance, if we are to have a relationship with our Higher Self, I believe that a healthy body is important. Our higher self is energy, and so is our body. If our body is sick or tired as a result of too many toxins or overwork then it is less likely to be able to make that connection.

Faith

You are unlikely to connect to Source, if you have little or no faith.

Doubt sees the obstacles, Faith sees the way.
Doubt sees the darkest night, Faith sees the day
Doubt dreads to take a step, Faith soars on high
Doubt questions 'Who believes?' Faith Answers I."

— *Unknown*

Faith is knowing the future will be ok, whereas trust is letting it happen now.
Faith is an expression of gratitude for your relationship with the creator. Fear is a lack of faith in the creator. Faith is strength in knowing that what is to happen to you is what you need – not necessarily what you want!

INTROSPECTIONS AND PREPARATION

Your answers lie inside you. The answers to life's questions lie inside you. All you need to do is look, listen and trust.
— *Cherie Carter-Scott*

Prayer is when you talk to God. Meditation is when God talks to you.
— *Diana Robinson*

As good as prayer is, when you talk you don't learn and as this workbook is about knowing thyself, you must listen.

To help you with your process of getting to know yourself, you will make use of introspection.

One of my dictionaries says that introspection allows for one to examine one's thoughts and feelings or observations of one's mental processes, i.e. how you react to certain situations. The clarity you derive gives a sense of calm and direction.

Introspection is a most natural and easy process of special awareness.

Stilling the Mind

Your mind is a kaleidoscope of crazy mixed up thoughts that bombard you all day. For any real contemplation to take place you need to *shut the mind up* for the time of introspection. Throughout this book I give you tools to do just that. Meditation, contemplation or deep relaxation is a method of allowing you to 'just be' without interference of random thoughts. It is also a method of **plain and simple thinking**. It is a process of focusing your thoughts on any subject you chose to clarify.

Once your mind is still and you apply your attention to the subject at hand, you will be amazed at what transpires. The insights you gain when you penetrate beyond the noise of your mind will startle you. For example, by focusing on the feeling that is the result of guilt you will dissipate it. Yes you will, or at least it will be reduced. The feeling of guilt is likely to return but when it does, you have the tool to 'go in' and dissolve it once again. By doing so on a regular basis you will find that each time you 'go in', it will take less time to reduce the guilt, which will return for shorter periods. When you focus on the guilt, <u>you will get to know what it feels like.</u>

STOP
Does it feel like butterflies or a dull pain?
Where does the guilt sit, in your stomach or your heart - where?

Make your notes..
....
....
....
....

Once you know what the guilt feels like, you will realise that it is an old companion, one you have been toting around for years. By having the awareness of where it sits, you can diminish it.

Remember that guilt is created by an accumulation of experiences. By using this tool to diminish it, you will also improve your ability to manage your thoughts. As a result you will become more positive in your day-to-day actions.

Let's assume that an issue you are concerned about resulted from an argument. The clarity you gain from introspection will be of great benefit. You will see your part in the argument, whether you were realistic or not. You will gain a better understanding of the other person's perspective and therefore a way forward. Or maybe you have a decision to make - to have a relationship or not, or to accept a job offer. Total focus is like running a movie in your head. You are able to see all the options clearly and gain understanding as a result. There will be many insights that never occurred to you before, insights that are brought to your attention by your Higher Self.

Norman Vincent Peale (theologian and writer) offered the opinion, "Only a quiet mind can think at maximum efficiency."

On reflection and some of the great religions

Introspection is a form of meditation. Some Christians may be wary of the idea of meditation. However, the KJ V: 01 of the Bible discusses the benefits and need to meditate on no less than twenty occasions. In fact all the major religions have been propagating the virtues of meditation for hundreds of years. They unanimously refer to the "stillness within".

I have more understanding than all my teachers, for your testimonies are my meditation.   - Psalm 119:99

In returning and rest shall ye be saved.   - Isaiah 30:15

In tranquillity, in stillness, in the unconditioned, in inaction, we find the levels of the universe, the very constitution of Tao.
*   - Chuang-Tse, 3rd Century Taoist*

Meditation is a form of prayer that goes beyond words and into the void.

Are you willing to try meditation as a form of prayer? ……………………………………
………………………………………………………………………………………………………
………………………………………………………………………………………………………
………………………………………………………………………………………………………
………………………………………………………………………………………………………
………………………………………………………………………………………………………

Supreme bliss surely cometh to the sage whose mind is thus at peace.
— *Bhagavad Gita*

Suddenly is the soul oned to God when it is truly peaced in itself.
— *Julian of Norwich*

A peaceful mind is your precious capital.
— *Sivananda*

Only in stillness, does one have the truth.
— *Shankaracharya*

Other Benefits of Introspection

If you introspect for twenty minutes daily, you will require less sleep, look and feel younger, reduce stress and develop a calmness that you are unlikely to have experienced before. You will feel closer to your Source because in stillness you strengthen the thread that connects you to "your Creator".

Believe that higher forces try to reach and help you. Allow them to succeed by dropping all mental barriers.

Your mental walls are the only obstructions that obstruct Truth's constant messages of help. The key to this is to silence the mind.
— *Unknown*

In our chaotic world where we have been taught to equate inaction with being lazy, many people have difficulty 'doing nothing' but it is in the stillness of the body and mind that we find answers, that our energy levels increase and that our lives become more balanced and productive.

Don't be put off by the fact that you are tempted to fidget or get distracted. After some practice, meditation will become your favourite source of relaxation and comfort.

Through introspection, for once you are giving more to the soul than to the body.

In preparation for introspection

The Four Brain Waves that influence our State Of Mind

Beta State is the state your brain waves are in during your normal day-to-day activities. It is the fastest brain wave.

Theta State is the state experienced during sleep (REM state) and during deep meditation when the person loses all sense of the physical body functions such as breathing and heartbeat. Digestion is slowed down immensely.

Delta State is the slowest brain wave. It is experienced in very deep sleep or when the mental and physical planes have been transcended.

For our purpose it is between alpha and theta that we will be working in.

Alpha State is the level your brain is in while you are sleeping, during meditation or when you are lost in creative thought. The brain activity is slowed down and you begin to access your subconscious mind.

Be aware of the following:

Invasive thoughts will be diminished and removed with patience and focus.
Allow time for the introspection; twenty minutes is usually enough.
Be prepared for anything to pop into your mind. Know that you are safe and that nothing will happen to you. When you 'introspect' you must let go and relax.
When you are relaxed you open yourself to the dropping down into the Alpha state of mind.
It is only when you are in the alpha state that you will be most effective in your introspection.

To prepare yourself for the ideal mental state for introspection, I suggest you carry out the following:

Make sure you will not be disturbed and the room you are in is quiet and has plenty of fresh air. See that you are comfortable, either sitting or lying on the floor. Close your eyes.

Thoughts will come to you while in introspection that you may want to remember later on. Have a pen and paper ready to jot these down immediately you come out of the Alpha state. You may want to use a Dictaphone to record your thoughts.
By slowing down your breathing, you slow down the thoughts that bombard your mind. You also lower your brain waves. When you reach the Alpha level, your mind will be calm with fewer intrusive thoughts. Your mind will be more receptive to focusing on your process and the receiving of relevant information.

You will now do your first introspection

Slow your breathing down and once you seem calmer take your mind to a quiet place (a place in nature perhaps), a place without fear, a place without responsibilities. Keep focused on this blissful place.

Starting the Process

Take six deep breaths and consciously release tension with each out breath. The deep breathing informs your mind that you are about to enter the Alpha state. Only later do you slow your breathing down.

Take your focus to your body. Start with your feet and work up (one step at a time) to the crown of your head. Relax each foot, each leg, buttocks, etc. Slowly does it. Spend time on relaxing your shoulders and face, both of which retain a lot of tension. The process should take about five minutes.

When at the crown of your head take two more deep breaths and sigh out any tension.

Tell yourself that you are going deeper into relaxation.

At this stage, consciously slow down your breathing and reduce your breath to that of a mere whisper.

When you feel yourself relaxed tell your mind you are going deeper and say, "With each breath I am more relaxed," while at the same time taking a few more breaths.

See yourself at the top of a staircase with ten steps. Gently descend one step at a time. Starting from the top, count backwards: "Ten, I am going deeper into relaxation, nine, I am going deeper into relaxation," until you reach the bottom.

See yourself walking to another set of steps and do the same again while affirming that you are going deeper.
Now you are ready to visualise yourself in the process of working through your chosen topic.

Ask for clarity and relief, while every so often reminding yourself that you are going deeper.

If the topic is one where you would like to change a mind-set, such as, 'I am confident at work'. See yourself in your work situation oozing confidence. How do you feel being confident? How do your colleagues view your new confident self? Immerse yourself in the experience, while repeating 'I am confident at work' at least ten times.

When you are ready, slowly count yourself out from one to ten as your breathing returns to normal.

Become aware of your body and surroundings, moving your fingers and wriggling your toes.

As you open your eyes, take note of your new refreshed and invigorated state.

Record your impressions: ....
....
....
....
....
....

Points to remember

There is no hurry. Be patient and go easy on yourself, especially with painful issues. You may need several sessions for a specific topic.

If external thoughts become intrusive, calmly allow them to flow through and out of your mind.

Tackle one topic per session.

If you feel yourself slipping out of the Alpha and back into the Beta state, repeat the last two steps of descending the staircase, while affirming that you are relaxing to a deeper level.

If peripheral thoughts associated with your process emerge, follow them and take them to their final conclusion. Then return to the core issue.

At the end of each session, describe your findings in your journal.

Try and do the session at the same time each day. This is your time and if you are consistent it will become easier.

To begin with your mind may wander. Like a young colt it will resist harnessing. Some days will be easier than others. Be patient with yourself, remain calm and determined. Like any skill, you will get better with practice. I assure you the effort will be worth it.

To change negative modes of behaviour, you need to repeat positive affirmations at least ten times per session.

Record future topics that you want to work with: ....

....
....
....
....
....
....
....
....
....
....

TOOLS FOR PROCESSING and how to work through your chosen topics

As you introduce a topic, don't look for answers straight away. Just get a feel for the subject. Your mind will get on with it in its own good time. Let it search for everything it knows about the subject and allow it to linger and massage the topic as required. Go slowly and methodically.

N.B. An important aspect of introspection is 'the feeling' you get when you ponder a subject. Take cognisance of 'the feeling'. Is the feeling one of guilt, anger, hate or remorse? Which area of the body does the feeling sit in? There may be times, when a topic of introspection will be so uncomfortable you may not be able to handle it. If so, **back off a bit** and think about the uncomfortable feeling. The next time you introspect, reintroduce the subject and you will probably be able to dig a little deeper. In time, you will be able to examine and feel it without any anguish. When that happens, you know the process is working and you are healing that aspect.

You will know when you have done enough. Gradually bring your breathing to normal and return to the awareness of your surroundings.

Lists

Make a list of all the issues that you want to clear through meditation. Your list could include many of the concepts that you will learn about in 'Know ThySelf'. However, some may be your own personal 'issues' that require your immediate attention.

Your lists: ....

....

....

....

....

Other thoughts? ....

....

....

....

....

....

....

Internalising and Changing Thought Processes

I have been meditating for twenty years and have tried many methods from guided meditations to mantras. They all have their place and are very good for specific purposes. However, if you want to influence your mind to make it work for you, I recommend the above method. Techniques that do not examine your issues will not clear them. You will feel great while in the meditation but when you come out the guilt, fear and anger may return.

Reversing an Unhappy Ending (Neuro-Linguistic Programming (NLP) calls this 'Change Personal History')

If a past event has bothered you, it may be helpful to imagine a different ending or in the case of severe trauma, a completely different set of circumstances. For example, if you were raped, change the outcome and see yourself, not changing the events (as it did happen), but changing the feelings and pain that resulted from the event. During introspection, run the event as if you are watching a movie. Visualise the circumstances (and feel the feelings that go with it) as you would have wanted them to be, and finish off the visualisation with an uplifting ending. When you do this, you re-programme the mind and release your emotional attachments to the event.

LIFE LESSONS
Life is your most consistent and rewarding teacher

Lessons usually come in the form of painful events, experiences or ways of being. If we don't develop tools and methods for dealing with these challenging life-altering events, we tend to 'react' to our circumstances in the following ways:
- Becoming a victim, the persecutor, or the rescuer
- Developing low self-esteem
- Becoming fearful
- Using anger as a defence mechanism

STOP
The above methods are very important in the identification of your issues. When visualising, don't focus on these. Instead, focus on the opposite, that is, the good result, otherwise you further entrench the bad habits.

INTROSPECTION
Do you think that your life works? Could it be improved? Do any of the above indicators sound familiar to you?

Make yourself comfortable, still your mind into the Alpha state and for a ten-minute period, ask yourself if any of the above points apply to you. If so, which ones?

Write down what you discover ....

....

....

....

....

Experience can only be of use when you look at a happening from a different mindset or attitude. It is only when you can see what an experience taught you that you are already beyond the need for that lesson. If you have no clarity as to why something happened, you still have more to learn or understand.

STOP
Did you take note of that last point - that for a life to really work you need a relationship with God, but while retaining a positive mind-set? Does this make sense to you, or do you think it is rubbish? Record your thoughts in your journal.

....
....
....
....

DOES YOUR LIFE WORK?

Meet Zelda, who is attractive but not beautiful, slim and always laughing. On the outside she seems motivated and determined. Her friends say that she is vivacious. Zelda always has a task to do, money to make and a future to grasp. That's on the outside. The inside tells a different story. Her life does not work – she has little energy and her health could be better, there is no money in her bank account and her relationships with lovers and friends fluctuate from good to stormy. Yet, 'It was not my fault,' is her mantra.

On the outside she tries to be positive and do the best with what she has, '… besides, what other choice do I have? I can't help it if I am unlucky,' she tells all.

Zelda carries hurt and anger but this tends to be buried deep down and so she is not really aware of it. Because of a life that doesn't work, she has self-esteem issues, but again she is not really aware of these. Her life does not work because her hidden demons govern it. They rule her mind with an iron grip, telling her what to think or which emotion to express. Moreover, they sabotage her life on a daily basis.

Now Zelda's friend Wendy has a life that works. She is the same age as Zelda and comes from the same suburb, yet she does not have the worry lines on her face that Zelda has. Although not rich, she is financially comfortable and can afford a pleasant holiday every year. Her health is sturdy and her marriage of ten years seems to get better as time goes on. She likes her job as a manager but does not let it interfere with her home life. She is motivated and happy, which is more than can be said of Zelda. The only difference between Wendy and Zelda is that Wendy is clear on 'her issues' and has faced them. Zelda has never taken that responsibility and so she is in a constant state of disarray.

Other indicators of a life that doesn't work:

- *A person who is accident-prone.*
- *A predominant thought is, 'Why me?'*
- *Things just do not get done on time - there is always too much to do. This person's life is in chaos, but unlike the chaos theory, there is no organising power behind the chaos. These people are always rushed off their feet and are tired as a result. Because things don't go smoothly, panic sets in and they feel that they lose control.*

- *Some people lunge from one catastrophe to another, three steps forward and four backwards. Lots of catastrophes are strong indicators of a life that doesn't work. There is always something keeping them down.*
- *Tomorrow it'll be better. You have heard that one, which means avoiding responsibility for today and hoping that tomorrow will be different. That is codswallop, as it is what you do today that will influence your tomorrow.*

The indications of a life that doesn't work go on and on, but I am sure you get the picture.

Our lives are a mixture of tempests and tranquillity, of good and bad, love and hate. Because of our human 'issues', we lose faith in the Universe to help, guide and provide for us. By remaining grounded in our material world and at the same time accessing our spiritual selves we achieve balance. When we are spiritually aware and clear, we open up blockages. The aim is to be close to The Divine, yet at the same time to know how to manage our life on a human material level.

Therefore, you need a positive attitude, while retaining a relationship with The Source.

Does your life work? ....
....
....
....

I believe we are able to have an ongoing relationship with God – The Source. I also believe that God is benevolent. If you discover this relationship, your life will be fantastic.

INTROSPECTION

Once in your Alpha state, bring to mind the indications of a life that does not work. Ascertain what does not work in your life. Look at each issue in turn and try to understand when each started, how much it affects your life, how often it bites you.

Journal: ....
....
....
....

I cannot emphasise enough that your spiritual development and human evolution go hand in hand. It is virtually impossible to resolve your human issues without faith.

So this is what KTS is all about; it is finding yourself and your place in the universe, i.e. <u>find yourself and you find God</u>.

The following is a good example of the difference between a functioning and a non-functioning life.

A universe, as explained by Collins English Dictionary: all existing things considered as constituting a systematic whole, and by The Concise Oxford Dictionary: all existing things, the whole creation (& the creator), all mankind combined into one whole. The Latin word universe means 'all in one, whole'.

A few weeks ago the hot water system in my house developed a slow leak, so I called in a plumber. He said that as it was old it would need to be replaced. If it wasn't replaced the leaking would get worse. He gave me a quote and we booked a date to do the work.

Now, totally unbeknown to me, the insurance company that insures my house had a change of policy, one for the better. They added sundry household repairs to their list of claimable items and fortunately for me, this included hot water systems. But here is the interesting part. The afternoon before the plumber was to come to do the work, I received a letter from the insurance company informing me of this new added service. I phoned the plumber to cancel and explained that the replacement hot water system is covered by my insurance policy and that they would supply their own plumber.

If this was to happen to a habitually negative person, for example, Zelda, the letter would have arrived the day <u>after</u> the hot water system had been installed and the money had already been paid to the plumber. Or the hot water system would have sprung the leak a week before the insurance company's commencement date of the new policy. Does this sound familiar to you?

The above example s typical of a positive life; how this actually works may be a mystery but it does work. I know because I have lived both.

Some people may say that it was 'lucky' that the letter came the day it did, but in reality a life that does not work is without luck and one that does work attracts luck.

STOP
Take the time to think about this last sentence. Think about people that you know whose life seems to work and it is likely that you will see that there is a certain amount of luck attached. Now for people whose lives don't work, how often have you heard the following, "When you are down, the boot goes in"?

Journal notes: ....
....
....
....
....

Habit

We are all where we are in life because of habits. A life that does not work is a life that is one of bad habits - bad thought habits. If we can change the habits, then clearly life will change.

Success has the affect of attracting more success and failure tends to attract more failure. Both are the result of habits - thought habits. The person who fails has a habit of negative thoughts and the person who has abundance is generally a habitual thinker of positive thoughts.

Fear is a habit, doubt is a habit, as is a belief that we are not good enough. Love for humanity is a habit.

To overcome bad habits, you must feed the mind with positive thoughts which grow to be beneficial habits.

STOP
Do a contemplation and try to see the link between
aspects of life that do not work for you, and your habits.

Journal notes: ....
....
....
....
....

It's not so much what you consume, it is what consumes you that counts. What bad habits consume you?

Have the courage to face your ghosts

So you can see that I teach from a position of empathy, throughout this workbook I have literally slit myself open from head to toe, exposing the entire contents of who I am, allowing my entrails to flop onto the floor. You can apply my history to help you with your life.

Throughout this book there are many snapshots of my life *(all in italic)*. You will see the events that directed it - such as the early departure of Hildegard, my biological mother, being shut up in an outside toilet, being dyslexic, spending time in an orphanage and other incidents.

Snapshot of Pat Grayson – Age 2.5 years old

The departure of my mother
Although I do not remember the circumstances surrounding my mother's departure, I am sure that I absorbed much.

The story as told by my Father was that she left him, taking my brother John and me with her. However, it was only a few days later he heard a car coming along the seldom-used dirt road and he went out to investigate. He saw a car that he didn't recognise stop at the gate. In the passenger's seat was his wife Hildegard, our mother. He saw an unknown man, who was the driver and our two little heads just above the window line.

The man was assumed to be the boyfriend. Apparently Hildegard turned around and reached over the front seat to open the back door and shooed John and I out. Our satchels soon landed unceremoniously in the dirt. No words were exchanged, just anxious looks. Then the car took off in a cloud of dust. We never saw her again. It was likely that the boyfriend did not want 'troublesome' kids, and so we were dispatched back to Dad.

Snapshot - Age 2.5 to 3

After Hildegard left, Dad was unable to look after two little ones and so we were shunted off to some friends of his. They lived on a farm and the following snapshot is something that I wrote to honour my brother.

My Brother John

It was only years later that I ascribed my daydreaming to The German who used to lock me in the dunny for hours on end.

Dunny is a lovely Australian word, meaning an outside toilet. This dunny, like all dunnys of the period, was a small hut, invariably made with wooden slats and a tin roof. All dunnies seemed to have rickety doors and spider webs in the corners. Dunnies were far enough away from the house so that an incoming breeze would not spoil meals, yet not so far that it was a 'trek' - who wants to wake up at night, in the middle of winter, and traipse kilometres up the garden?

Yes, after Mom absconded, Dad left my brother and me in the not too good care of a countryman of his. I call him The German because, as I was only three at the time, I cannot remember his name. So we stayed with him and his family on their farm out back of Sydney.

The German did not like me and took great delight in demonstrating this. One of his favourite pastimes was to lock me in the dunny whenever he went out. While I was incarcerated, my brother John was given strict instructions not to let me out - otherwise he would regret it. Knowing The German, John was too petrified to buck the command.

I remember one such time; perhaps it was not just one time but all the times that a small child rolls into one. I must have sat in that box all day. To start with, slithers of sunlight shone through the slats from behind me. Many daydreams later, they were in my face, with dust particles dancing in the shafts of light.

I sat on the closed seat, as otherwise, being just a little thing, I would have fallen in. The wood became hard after a while and hurt my bum. Of course, there was no food and no water. I don't recall what went through my mind as the hours passed. I do however, remember my brother. Not once would he leave my side or rather, the side of the dunny. If I was about three he would have been five. We did not talk, as he was the silent type. But, if suddenly I would say, 'John, are yer there?' there would always be the reassuring answer, 'Yeah.' His support was my solace.

Two hours later: 'John, yar there?' 'Yeah Pat, I are'. He never wandered away or faltered in his vigilance to support his little brother. How my five-year-old brother took on this duty I will never know, but I'll always be grateful. As an adult reflecting on it, I think that in many ways, John's burden was worse than mine.

These memories are my earliest and probably stick because of their profundity.

A year or so later, it was John who supported me while we were in the orphanage. He was my personal guardian angel, always there, not saying much but always a strong presence.

More years passed and he was still there, a silent support system. We grew up and how sad I was when the day came, and as a man of fifteen my brother John joined the navy. He was heading to the other side of the country, some 3,500 kilometres away.

Now, 48 years later, I still feel the tears prickling my eyes when I recall John aboard a train, called The Spirit of Australia, as it detached itself from the station and pulled him ever faster away from me.

We have to be brave to work through our human issues and problems, but remember you are not given any inadequacies that you can't handle.

If your life is unduly hard, it is probable that you will challenge the benevolence of The Creator. You may think, 'It either does not exist or it has forsaken me.'

Some people may quit this workbook and think, '*Gee, I don't need to do this*'. But what they are really doing is avoiding their issues. They dare not investigate the cause of their anger *or* want to face their fear.

Most people (including myself) are secure in the comfort zones of their imperfections. We do not want to rock the boat and wet our security blankets for the sake of self-improvement. Complacency induces smugness and a false sense of satisfaction. It is easier to do nothing than to do something - especially change. Most are not ready for mental emancipation.

Look at the following three quotations on how we avoid searching deep within ourselves.

Nothing in the world is more distasteful to a man than to follow the path that leads to himself.
- *Hermann Hesse, 1877 - 1962*
(writer, pacifist and opponent of Hitler)

The truth that makes men free is for the most part the truth which men prefer not to hear. - *Herbert Agar*

It's a rare person who wants to hear what he doesn't want to hear.
- *Dick Cavett*

STOP
Record your impressions of these quotations in your journal.
How do you feel about the prospect of stirring
the embers of your painful past?

Journal notes: ....
....
....
....
....

Challenge Your Current or Inherited beliefs

As children growing up we are fed with beliefs. For us to evolve these must be challenged. The love that this book offers will inspire you to challenge all that you currently know or think you know, and all that you think you understand.

Rome charged Galileo with heresy for suggesting that the world was round instead of flat. Galileo was not afraid to challenge the established ideas of the time. The same applies to Socrates. He was forced to drink poison because his precepts were not in line with those of the authorities. Apparently Socrates did this calmly and without remorse. Certainly you will not have to drink poison but it is wise to challenge your own and other people's beliefs - including mine.

> **STOP**
> **How can you challenge your current beliefs**
> **if you don't know what they are?**

....
....
....
....
....
....
....
....
....
....

Snapshot – Age 2.5 to 4 'You sit and vatch the train'

A memory that I have from my time on the farm was when The German placed John and me at the edge of the property. This was adjacent to a rail line. We were told to "Sit and vatch the train." This would have been fun if trains came past, but in all the time that I was there not one did, nor was there a toot-toot, a choo-choo or anything that resembled a train.

I was so little I sat with my legs straight along the ground and back vertical, yogi like. Flowers with yellow heads and grass reached to my chest and fluttered in the breeze. I pulled at them.

It was then it happened - a butterfly floated past and as it did my focus floated with it. In no time I was up and after it.

Seconds later I heard the screech of the fly-screen door opening and then slamming shut. The German covered the ground from the kitchen to me in no time. Slap, cuff, and push as I was hit on the head and dumped to the ground with the raging words, "I told you to sit still. I told you to vatch the trains." Clearly he knew that this toddler's concentration would lapse and so the blighter sat there waiting to pounce. The hitting did not hurt me but as little as I was I knew that there was an injustice to it and felt feelings of inadequacy and helplessness.

I said earlier that people are scared to delve too deeply - they would rather be secure in their insecurities than happy. Of course this decision is largely subconscious. But essentially, people are scared to scratch and when they are at the psychologist, they skirt around topics, but they won't own them.

Challenge your current beliefs ……………………………………………………………………
………
………
………
………

Sometimes you can ignore how a problem arose, accept it, move on and it works out fine. But more often than not, you have to search to find out what the underlying problems are. Some time during the process you need to take responsibility for how long you have allowed a problem to rule you.

When it comes to resolving past issues which influence your current thought processes, there are four basic steps:

The first is to take responsibility, accepting that there are issues governing certain modes of dysfunctional behaviour in your life; behaviour patterns that could be detrimental to your wellbeing and happiness.

Secondly, you need to understand the issue and know where it comes from and how it affects you. For instance, I learnt about forgiveness and so I forgave 'The German', who set the course of my life. For a time, I thought that's all I needed to do to be clear. But I did not become clear and I still had a dysfunctional life. The reason was that a belief that **'I was not good enough'** was set in place. It was only after bringing this into conscious thought that I was able to dismantle its influence.

The third step is one of action. You really need to expose yourself to the pain - understanding the feelings that come with it, i.e. sadness, guilt, feeling dirty, etc. When you understand and *feel it*, the hurt will start to subside. Or when you know what it feels like, you will recognise those feelings as soon as they arise. You will be able to work on it, before it works on you. Later, under the section on fear and guilt, I talk about the feeling of squirming snakes in my belly.

The fourth step is to realise that to totally eliminate an issue, you may need to repeat the first three phases over a period of time. Remember that healing is a process and not a quick fix.

If you merely talk about your issues, you are intellectualising them. You have to go deeper (experiential). If we look at the base for the words psychology and psychiatry, the word psyche is defined as soul, spirit and mind. Intellectualising is beneficial but doesn't get to the psyche or soul.

I have read that 'the conscious mind is only 10% of our total mind'. Therefore, we have another 90% available to access. What is hidden is the unknown (the psyche). For complete healing we need to solve problems on a soul level. This book has tools which offer thoughts to intellectualise and methods to actualise.

My path was shaped from my very earliest days, by events that had the effect of taking away my power. Being very young, a script or pattern was formed in my mind that I was powerless and so my life progressed with that belief. I had no control over Hildegard leaving, nor could I stop myself from being locked in the dunny. There was nothing I could do about the abuse that was meted out, nor the lack of care in the orphanage or the other episodes in my life that I refer to later on in the book.

It took many years and a lot of work to reach out and forcefully grab back my power, to hold it close to my chest, never again to escape. Since then, it has grown strong and unequivocal. If you listen and apply the messages of this work, you will also be in a position to reclaim your power.

INTROSPECTION

Once you have composed yourself, reflect on the events that shaped who you are. Once again record your findings.

Journal notes: ....

....

....

....

STOP
**Write down in your journal what you consider
to be some of your issues.**

Journal notes: ....

....
....
....
....

Snapshot – Age 10

There was a long period where I felt so inadequate, that I wanted to be someone else. I would think of a classmate and wish that somehow I could become him and that he would take over the wasteland that I was.

Ongoing Work

From reading this book, it might appear that I am smart and wise, that I 'have arrived'. Far from it. I am fallible. As enlightened as I may be in certain areas, I still make mistakes and I hurt on occasions.
The task of life enhancement must be free of blame and we must be gentle on ourselves. We must be vigilant in our desire to heal. There need be no remorse for things past and no worry about events in the future. I have travelled a long way down this road and would never want to return to the starting point. I will continue to stride forward along this path in confidence that the further along I go the better my life becomes.

STOP
Are you ready to take this giant step,
a step that will hurt on occasions?

....
....
....
....
....

The ramblings of a writer - changing your circumstances but not your mindset?

Can you imagine leaving your home to go somewhere else to adopt a new persona, where you pretend to be someone different, rather like Clark Kent turning into Superman? You think that you will gain instant happiness. So you change your clothing, take on a different hairstyle and speak with a posh accent. You may start the process at the local hotel of your new town and act as if you are someone else. Someone wiser or richer, perhaps more confident than who you really are. Later you walk or stagger out feeling smug and believing that you have really impressed the audience.

It may be fun for a while but like a bubble finding its way to the surface, the way you saw yourself in your old life will emerge into the new. You may look and sound different but the insecurities will be the same. The excitement of the new life and friends will diminish whilst your original fears reassert themselves.
Excitement about the new life and friends will diminish while your original fears reassert themselves. Your strengths will remain strengths and your weaknesses will be just as prominent, irrespective of how many times you 'Clark Kent' yourself. The philosophies and beliefs that were collected throughout your life will still assert themselves in all conversations with your newly acquired friends. Your loves, hates and prejudices about God, man and country will cling to your being, like fleas cling to a dog.

The 'acting out' of a new life would, like yesterday's coat of paint, fade. The way you see yourself will place you with a new set of friends but friends much the same as those left behind. You would attract similar circumstances into the new life that you may be running from. You remain who you are because of the way you see yourself. You can't change yourself by external trimmings. You have to change from within. It can be a slow process, much the same as chipping away at raw granite until an approximation of who you want to be remains.

But unlike perfect art, we are never finished. We are always a work in progress. We can't run away from what we have become, but we can grow towards what we want to be.

Yes, perhaps it could be fun being someone else in a new town or country but that's all we would be – someone else. Our little selves will still cry out and say, "Here I am, please see me!"

INTROSPECTION

Once you are composed, feel gratitude for who you are and what you have in your life – your loved ones, health, job, your dogs and cats and any other influential assets. For the time of the introspection, feel grateful and privileged.
Try to carry that gratitude with you throughout the rest of your day.

Journal: ………………………………………………………………………………………
………………………………………………………………………………………………..
………………………………………………………………………………………………..

....
....
....
....
....
....

CONCEPTS

Within this work there are words, phrases and concepts that are subjective. I therefore use my own definitions. You may disagree with them. However, the concepts throughout the book are based on my understanding. Let's start with the biggest one and that is The Supreme Being or God.

Supreme Being

There are many words for The Supreme Being - yours depends on what religion or culture you were raised in. God is the Christian term and is also used by Jews. I could equally use Tao if I were Chinese, Allah (Islam), Brahman (Hinduism). These religions teach that there is only one Supreme Being.

It is impossible to describe the Supreme Being. How can we describe something that we do not understand, something we may feel but haven't touched? The Supreme Being is all around us, it is in and a part of us, yet if I ask you to pass me a little bit of Supreme Being, just a smidgen, you couldn't.

We cannot describe The Supreme Being. How can we when as humans we are not equipped to understand the grandness of it all? The Koran says, **"No vision can grasp Him"**.

It is for this reason I give you some of the titles bestowed upon the Supreme Being from different religions and cultures: The Supreme, The Source, Absolute Consciousness, Absolute Truth, Holy Spirit, Inner Nature of Man, The Creator, Universal Intelligence or Creative Intelligence, Divine Spirit, Be-All, Most High, Universal Spirit, Universal Energy, Higher Consciousness, Collective Consciousness (Carl Jung), Higher Self, Ruler of The Universe, Supreme Intelligence, The All That There Is and sometimes it is called That or even It. In Native America it is called the Void.

Although the above words describe the Supreme Being, there is to me an extra connotation and that is that He/She/It is benevolent and caring. It does not matter what you call It, you are a part of Its universal intelligence. Rumi of the Sufi tradition called It, **"The Master of Existence"**.

STOP
In your journal, write down what the Universal Source means to you.
Be careful to use your own thought-through concepts and not the spoon fed ideas you were given when you grew up.

Journal ....

....

....

....

The Higher Self = our connection to all that there is

The Higher Self is that part of us which is Godlike. It is the opposite of our personality, our behaviour, our ego.

The Higher Self can only be felt or understood once you reduce the mind clutter. It is only with a quiet mind that you create a receptacle that allows you to see something of the Higher Self. You have done this on occasions throughout your life. It may have been when you were in awe of a starry night sky or when your first child was born. It could have been while out in nature, perhaps on a hike, where you felt 'it.' Yes, you have felt your Higher Self, but that part of you which you know as your Higher Self is only the thin edge of the wedge. There is much more. By taking the time to listen, you will get to know and understand your Higher Self. This sets yogis and ascetics on their path. When you find your Higher Self you are as close to God as you can get as a human being.

Because we have families and responsibilities we cannot all become yogis, nor would we all want to. But we can travel towards understanding with just a few minutes of consciousness per day.

Having that awareness and shutting off the mental clutter will help you access your Higher Self. The sections on introspection will help you to do this.

STOP
Have you ever wondered why you should
bother to know your Higher Self?

....
....
....
....

One answer is that you cannot know your Higher Self without knowing who you are. When you know your Higher Self you have a greater respect and reverence for life. The Higher Self is that part of you that provides your intuition, your quiet wisdom and compassion. When you have an affinity to your Higher Self you will learn to trust life and learn things that you never thought possible.

Divine Principles
Throughout this book I mention The Divine or the Divine within you. What I mean by this is that your higher self is your natural birthright.

The Bible says that man is made in God's image. If this is the case, and I believe it is, then by grasping the Divinity within, we are accessing the spirit of God.
When I say that you are made in the image of God, I don't really know what that means as I don't know what God is, but certainly we are an aspect of the all that there is.

Heaven

Heaven is not 'out there', it is within – you make your own heaven.

Spirit

The Concise Oxford Dictionary describes Spirit as 'the intelligent or immaterial part of man or soul'. It refers to a person's mental or moral code or qualities, 'spiritual' as opposed to matter, as acted on by Supreme Being.

The word 'spiritual' often appears in the book. It refers to that part of man that is not man (as opposed to matter) and the qualities of the Higher Self as in soul.

What is Spirituality?

It is not 'New Age.' New Age merely offers hints and directions. Don't look for it in the trappings of religion; focus on the inner meaning of love for your fellow man. Spirituality is our path to God, a direct and uncomplicated open door to the Creator. Spirituality is not ritual or candle burning, although as preparation to compose yourself for God, it can be beneficial. Spirituality is trust and faith. It is belief that God is there and there, here and within you. It is you, not separate, nor distant. Faith extends to the knowledge that God is benevolent and as we want the best for ourselves, so does God. It is we humans who separate God from us. We are the perpetrators of our own aloneness, not abandoned, just isolated from Source. It takes little effort to embrace All That There Is but a massive attitudinal shift. When it comes to God, simplify all, cut through the rubbish, see God in trees, as God is the trees. It is also the cow and the river. Nor is it necessary to go to church, a mosque, an ashram or temple to find It, as It permeates all of nature.

INTROSPECTION

Let's feel a little bit of our divinity. Go into your introspection mindset and focus on nothing other that the connection to 'All That There Is'. Focus on the void, the nothing.

Once you have composed yourself, look with your inner eye at the dark space behind your eyes (between your eyebrows) - just focus on this point. After a time you will feel a connection.

It is a wonderful feeling, one that you can create anytime you want. In fact, you don't even need to go into the Alpha state, all it takes is to allow yourself the time to focus and connect.

Journal: ....
....
....
....
....
....

Benevolent or not benevolent

Throughout this work it is seldom that I disparage any of the main religions but I am going to do so now. The Hasid and the Christians (through the Old and New Testament) teach that God is to be <u>feared</u>. This could not be further from the truth. Once you have the relationship with The Source that I suggest is possible, you will see that I am right and that God is benevolent. God being love cannot also be something to be feared.

Religion

<u>Pocket Oxford's definition is as follows</u>: 'Belief in superhuman controlling power, especially in a personal God or gods entitled to obedience and worship; expression

of this in worship; particular system of faith and worship; thing that one is devoted to; life under monastic vows.'

And now follows my interpretation on religion

Religion is a set of rules, defined and written by man as an instruction on how to, or not to, worship The Supreme Being. It invokes ritual and control and has very little to do with The Supreme Being or the seeking of The Divinity within.

Religion suggests that you go to 'The Creator', via man in manmade structures. I believe in Spirituality that teaches how to feel The Divine, to experience it, to live it, to be it. We need to look beyond the manmade issues, to the real matter.
Let me give you an example, for several years I enrolled at a local "School of Philosophy". It was great, I learnt about Socrates and Plato. I also learnt a smattering of Sanskrit and concepts such as the 'present moment'. I loved it, but something was missing and an obvious something. The missing component was God and a profound intimacy with It. There was no reaching out. It was all theory. The same applies to most religions, where there is so much emphasis on the trappings and not the *being with God*. There is no silencing yourself to be with Him, to feel Him and live your life with Him. So many people go to church or a religious ceremony to clear their conscience – not to be with God -- and in this way they shun their own responsibility.

I am sorry if I offend you. You may be very devout in what you believe and be very knowledgeable about the Bible or the Koran, but have you ever felt that something was missing? I guess what I am really trying to say is that you take responsibility for your relationship with the Universal Source and get closer to 'It' regardless of any restrictions placed on you by manmade dogma.

I have no doubt that there are times when some services are profound and God touches all who are there. You may walk out filled with love. That is beautiful but the point is that you can feel this love within you all the time - if your allow yourself the mantle of being spiritual, as apposed to understanding your religion on an intellectual level and experiencing it once a week or whenever you attend a religious gathering.

STOP
**Did you feel challenged when you read the above comments on religion? If so, record the reasons why.
Take the time to ponder them. The most important thing is for you to be clear on your religious beliefs and understand the difference between religion and being spiritual.**

Journal: ………………………………………………………………………………..

....
....
....
....

Spiritually is always, religion is occasional

Spirituality did not create The Holy Wars (just the term "Holy War" is a contradiction and oxymoron), pogroms or inquisitions. It is man in his folly of trying to assert rules and rituals that created those wars – using religion.

I do affirm that if your religion helps you to find the Divine within you, then it has served you well. Once you have accessed the God within you, you no longer need to get carried away by ritual or dogma.

Lastly, I would like to say that if you are Muslim, Christian, Jew, Hindu, Buddhist, if you practise Confucianism or any other creed, by being more spiritual it is likely that you will be a better Muslim, Christian, Jew, Hindu, Buddhist or Confucianist.

Einstein said: "All religions, arts & sciences are branches of the same tree. All these aspirations are directed toward ennobling man's life, lifting it, from the sphere of mere physical existence and leading the individual towards freedom."

Record you thoughts ....
....
....
....
....

My religion consists of a humble admiration of the illimitable superior spirit who reveals himself in the slight details we are able to perceive with our frail and feeble minds.
- Albert Einstein

As the book talks about spiritual concepts, I make it clear that it's non-religious. I believe that the main religions' core beliefs are basically the same. They are:

- There is one Supreme Being
- Love your fellow man
- God is within, not external to us
- Non-violence

The main purpose of most religions is to attain a closer loving relationship with The Supreme Being. For instance, the Muslim word Islam means, *submission to God*. Throughout the book, you will find quotes from all the major religions as well as my own definitions.

Either Good or Evil

Religions will divide you in into either evil or divine. Clearly they do not consider you divine. That would be asking too much. So therefore in the eyes of many religions you must be evil. You are born evil, you collect evil and although they in their high power of office allow you to repent of evil, you never get rid of it, as you always carry evil.

Being spiritual sees you as divine, not evil

If you think that life and what God allows to happen to you is unfair, then your life will be full of disappointments. If you accept that The Creator will cherish and nurture you and providing you remain of a positive nature then hooray, but it is up to you!

It is the Supreme Being's *will* that you have all of the fruits of life, such as in *our daily bread*, as the Lord's Prayer teaches. Once you understand and internalise this you make it easier for It to express Itself through you.

STOP
Find yourself and you find God.

Does the above statement ring true for you? ....
....
....
....

This book is about improving your life and so your call to action is by:

- Accessing your core issues and resolving them.
- Embracing the Divine within.

INTROSPECTION

When in a relaxed state, look at what God means to you.

Journal notes: ……………………………………………………………………..

………………………………………………………………………………………….

………………………………………………………………………………………….

………………………………………………………………………………………….

………………………………………………………………………………………….

………………………………………………………………………………………….

Karma

Karma is a Hindu and Buddhist philosophy and is normally understood to be the sum of a person's actions in all of his successive states of existence. Karma for the purpose of this book, suggests that what comes around goes around or that all our actions have consequences, every action has an equal or opposite reaction. Science may call it 'cause and effect'.

As humans, we must take responsibility for our actions and thoughts and must be prepared to accept the consequences. It is believed that we accrue Karma from previous lifetimes. For the purpose of this book, we are only going to concern ourselves with this lifetime, the here and now and our conscious memories. As far as I'm concerned, it is pointless worrying about past or possible future lives. It is like a Grade One pupil being concerned about exams for third-year university. Another way of understanding Karma is 'what you put out is what you get.'

Baggage

Baggage is a wonderful word that means gathering up all your negative issues from your recent or distant past and putting them into an imaginary bag that never leaves your side. If the bag left your body you could not extract each hurt or pain or imbue yourself with its agony afresh. Baggage carriers allow themselves to wallow in their remorse, reliving the bad episodes whenever they feel like pressing the replay button.

The baggage is their set conversation piece and becomes their persona - or does their persona become their baggage?

To make the baggage easier to transport, and so they can stuff it with more of their miseries, they attach stainless steel castor wheels to the bag. You will recognise the baggage people the minute you say, "Good morning, how are you?" Then you wish you had kept your mouth shut as they just don't know how to be happy.

A friend of mine felt that she needed a new beginning. She got divorced, moved into a new house, got new furnishings, bought new clothes, had a change of hair style and guess what? Same old rubbish, just a new day, because her baggage came with her – towed behind the removal truck on those shiny stainless steel castors!

> **STOP**
> We all carry *some* baggage. To recognise yours it will help to look for it in others. Take the time to think about the baggage carriers you know. Write about them. Then look for those traits within yourself.

....
....
....
....

> **STOP**
> Once again, as you did for baggage, look for your and other people's attachments. Write them down.

Your baggage traits...
....
....
....
....
....
....
....
....
....

Stuck

We allow ourselves to be afflicted with, 'being stuck' when we allow our issues to block our progress. We become stuck when we have an issue that we will not resolve or let go of. Other reasons for being stuck are fear, lack of belief in oneself or comfort zones.

You are the creator and releaser of your 'stuck' issues. Stuck things are the items that are in the baggage person's bag. The owners of a stuck thing have difficulty overcoming the issues and so remain stuck.

Attachments

Attachments are baggage items but with added emotion. You don't just have the recollection of a distressing event. You have the feeling, the vision and the pain in magnified detail. Like baggage, you also become stuck in a groove, unable to move on from it.

Journal notes: ....
....
....
....
....

Letting Go

Letting go is the grownup side of becoming UNSTUCK. It is letting go of the emotion or the attachment – the action involved with moving through and out of 'our familiar groove'.

Energy = God's petrol

We all know what energy is - or do we? Do you see energy? Can you pick it up or carry it home? If you look at your dictionary you will see about twenty lines describing an intangible. All of these would be true. The way the word 'energy', as used in this book, is to help describe Divine processes. It is a Divine force that is greater than we are. When it is used in this book, it has a spiritual connotation.

Realising The Self

Realising the self refers to the journey we undertake to master our lives. Of course achieving complete mastery is rare. It is the journey that is important as there is always new ground to break, new paths to travel and so we must not give up striving. Besides, giving up is not worth considering.
Take my life as an example, I had a choice. I could remain in a life that did not work, one of frustration and calamity, or find myself and my place in the Universe and grow

from there. When I was locked in the dunny as a toddler I had **no** choice. Striving for realisation of the self is a choice, but it is also a process.

Being On The Path (A Spiritual term)

You are on The Path when you are a sincere seeker for the answers of life. You cannot be on The Path without a relationship with the Creator.

Awareness, Being in the Present Moment or conscious living

The present moment is NOW, not something that happened last week or might happen next week. Not being in the present moment shows you are unaware of what is going on right this instant. When not in the present moment as per this definition, you have lost power and wasted time. Moreover, you will not move on, you'll remain stuck, frozen in the past. You will reduce your capacity to create your future because 'the lights are out on the top floor.' If you live each day as perfectly as you are able, you will ensure a perfect future. To live each day perfectly requires being in the *now*.
When you are not in the present moment, you miss many opportunities and experiences, like the scent of flowers or the wonder and beauty that surrounds you.

Best of all, when you are in the present moment you are closer to the Supreme Being. Try it now. Go out into the garden or to a park and just focus on where you are. You will know what I mean – you will start to understand my interpretation of spirituality.

The term 'present moment' is used extensively through the book.

Inner Self

Most of the time, our focus is external. For instance, it could be on earning money, (which is external) or on what we are to do on the weekend (also external), about our relationships (external) and so it goes on. Yet we only get to grips with who we are and how we fit in the grand scheme of things when we look at the inner journey. Another term for inner journey is being in the present moment.

Awareness

To remain in the inner self takes awareness. With patience and consistency you access the inner self.

How do you find God?

There is only one way and that is to slow down your mind and focus on the inner self. When your thoughts are external as given above, you will have created distance between you and God.

Victim

The following story taken from my own life experience is the perfect example of a childhood trauma that could have created a victim if I had allowed myself to perpetuate my issues.

Snapshot - Orphanage Bath Time

After the farm, John and I were put in an orphanage. Bath time in the orphanage was a study of mass production. There were two bathrooms adjacent to each other. These were small cubicles that only contained the bath and if they had doors they were never closed. We inmates approached the bathroom from two queues, one for girls and the other for boys. In each bath there was only one lot of water for all those in the queue and so if you were at the back, you could almost stand on the water as opposed to being in it! The production line moved in a steady progression – about every ninety seconds you took a step closer to the bath. Now remember I am an adult recalling events that happened when I was about four and so the timing and actual method may not be as represented but certainly the essence is correct.

There were two orderlies per bathroom. As you approached the door, the one orderly stripped you down. That happened in conjunction with another kid being washed in the bath. When this infant was deemed to be cleaner than when he started, he would be prodded to step out of the bath and the next one would step in. We sort of half squatted, whilst the second orderly ran a flannel over us as if to scour the dirt off. Roughly ninety seconds later the child was out the bath, dried and dressed.

One day I was in the queue, towards the back and was doing what all normal boys do - that is talk and have fun. This did not suit the undressing orderly who told me to keep quiet. I probably did, for only a minute or two but then forgot and started chirping again. Well I cannot remember what the orderly looked like, so I am going to improvise. It is likely she had a big bulbous nose that was red and lined with veins. A wart or two would have spotted her face and these had a small forest growing from them. She would have had a mouth that forgot how to smile some thirty years earlier and eyes that were too far apart. Eyes that bulged out in a frantic sort of way... Sorry, got carried away.

The wart came down the line and pushed me into the middle of the girls queue and told me that, "I would bath with them."

I had no sisters and knew nothing about girls, they were totally alien and I felt that I had been delivered into the hands of a strange species. I was acutely aware of my difference and I did not want to share those differences with them. I was mortified and wanted to disappear under that muddy water, never to resurface. The girls were equally embarrassed as they were also exposed to this male hooligan.

It amazes me that a person whose job is to care for children could be so insensitive.

A victim, as suggested in this book, is a person who feels that the world is against him or her, that there is some sort of conspiracy to hurt, belittle or generally be put down. These people are normally carriers of baggage and clearly do not take responsibility for themselves. If you are a victim and you are reading this, it is likely that you will think that this does not apply to you. Victims live in the past and blame the world for their woes. The problem is that they never work through their past.

> **STOP**
> **Identify some victims. Try and see how their lives would improve if they took a more proactive approach. Now look at yourself and see whether you are or have been a victim.**

Identify victims: ....
....
....
....
....
....

INTROSPECTION

For today, introspect on feeling good. Feel the warmth in your heart and allow it to radiate out from your body to embrace the world. Consciously hold the feeling long after you come out.

Journal: ....
....
....
....
....

LIFE'S PURPOSE = Moving closer to Source

Is there a purpose to our lives other than procreation? Of course! <u>We are here to find The Divinity within</u>. Once we find it, we have to utilise it in our lives. Once we find it, we can never lose it, but expressing it may be hard as life gets in the way.

Our humanness causes all sorts of impediments. We have rent or debts to pay, mistakes to rectify, mistakes to make, livings to earn, lessons to learn and so on.

Justice in Life

Dr Wayne Dyer in his best seller, 'Your Erroneous Zones' said it so well when he wrote, 'If the world was organised so that every thing was fair, no living creature could survive. Birds would be forbidden to eat worms, as it would not be fair to worms or for spiders to eat flies, etc.' This wonderful piece of wisdom shows you that there is no justice in the world. Dyer continues, 'Accept that life can be harsh, then get on with it. Too many of us demand that fairness be an inherent part of our lives. You moan, "It isn't fair" - "You have no right", etc. Don't use a lack of justice as justification for unhappiness. It is all part of life's process and if you accept this, then you will be better equipped to take responsibility for your life.

The Mystery of Life

You have just learnt that there is no justice in life. The next punch in the stomach is to learn that life is a mystery and no matter how much you grow and learn, it will never make sense to you. You will never know why there are wars or rape and hate - why innocent children get harmed and die. Some of it has got to do with the fact that there is no justice in life... but there I go again trying to understand the unknowable. A smattering of it can be explained by understanding the polarities in life, that everything has its opposite: love and hate, good and evil, light against dark. But it still does not explain the so-called injustices that we see all around us.

Part of grasping the meaning of life is to accept that you cannot be in control of events outside of yourself. You can't control something you don't understand. Getting frustrated with the mysteries of life will not help. You have to accept that there are some things you can't possibly have influence over and there are mysteries so far beyond your comprehension - and get on with it. Believe it or not, this manner of thinking gives you the freedom to overcome difficult times. Some things are best left in God's hands.

Krishnamurti, the Indian mystic, said, "Freedom from the desire for an answer is essential to the understanding of a problem."

Pleasures and limitations of mortality

Life is a paradox of opposites, a balancing act of pleasures and limitations. It's impossible to be happy without challenges, as challenges shape our mindset. Let's read that last sentence again: it's impossible to be happy without challenges as challenges shape our mindset. Pain can lead to growth, while pure pleasure leads to complacency. Without pain we would not be stirred to find ourselves or the Higher Power.

Techniques

There are techniques for living a life that is fun and gives contentment. The following are six suggested techniques for achieving that contentment:

1) Find people in your life to love. Give them as much love as you can and see yourself receiving more than you gave.

2) Simplify your life. Remove the clutter and slow it down. This will help to keep you balanced and clear.

3) Search for The Creator and have a relationship with It – life does not truly work without this relationship.

4) Do something creative. This can be a hobby, or a part of your employment. It must be a challenge and enjoyable. By doing so you will see that it will help you to find your place in the world.

5) Take time out for solitude (the introspections are perfect for this) – for clarity, calmness and balance.

6) Last, but certainly not least, learn to love yourself.

Start these techniques today and watch your life improve.

Who am I? Understanding polarity

When you learn what it is like to love and to hate, you will learn what polarity is (the opposite poles). When you experience the beauty of a sunset and the sadness of death. You will learn about emotions like fear and anger, you will learn about tears and that they are salty and what they signify.

Why the polarity? If you have learnt from everything you have ever experienced, that is both ends of the pole, it will be to answer the question, "*Who am I?*"

You have marvellous experiences, such as music that resonates to your inner soul and pets to show you unconditional love. You learn what it is like to fall so deeply in love with someone that you allow your energy to melt into his or hers. And you learn what it is like to have enemies who would gobble you up and annihilate you if you're not careful.

What a wonderful game life is. Yes, "Who am I?" All the experiences are designed to help you learn and to help you come to a new depth of understanding of "Who am I?" The answer is I AM A DIVINE BEING.

The Bible speaks of Life's processes in Ecclesiastes 3:1-8:

"To everything there is a season, and a time to every purpose under heaven: A time to be born, and a time to die; a time to plant and a time to pluck up that which is planted; a time to kill and a time to heal; a time to break down and a time to build up; a time to weep and a time to laugh; a time to mourn and a time to dance; a time to cast away stones and a time to gather stones together; a time to embrace and a time to refrain from embracing; a time to get and a time to lose; a time to keep and a time to cast away; a time to rend and a time to sew; a time to keep silent and a time to speak; a time to love and a time to hate; a time of war and a time of peace."

We live in a world of actuality, a real world of nature where animals, plants, insects and humans exist the hard way, and survive through the repetition of individual experiences. The drive for survival, the necessity for feeding ourselves and keeping alive in a real and cruel world, turns us into materialists, pessimists and realists. This is the world in which we have to labour, compete and struggle to earn our bread; a world that is greedy, immoral and seeks its own satisfaction.

Yet it is a world that can give us wonderful returns, returns based on our understanding of its harsh lessons. All life's harsh lessons are presented to us in an amazing choreography of events. If we learn the lessons, they normally disappear - but be aware as they may return from time to time to re-test us. Once they disappear, others are presented, which we also have to master.

As we go through life conquering the challenges and learning more, life gets better. If we choose to be blind to life's lessons, they will keep recurring at regular intervals, cloaked in different forms but the lessons will be the same.

I look at my life's process and see a wonderful series of events, from the difficult beginning, to my spiritual present where I know that I am looked after - from being a bricklayer to an entrepreneur, illiterate to being an author. Is that not growth? Is that not beautiful?

Every hurt, every anger, every relationship, all the disappointments as well as the happy times have made me who I am right now. It is not only the big events. It is the millions of little things that have happened in my life that have moulded my current character and the same applies to you.

STOP
Why do you think that the things that happened to me affected me as they did?

....
....
....
....
....

My life's work was to repair the damage, and as I did my self-esteem improved, as did my confidence.

Reaching For Our Divinity

How do we live our divinity? To start with, we are encouraged to live with more awareness. Another source of help is to reduce the number of aggravations within our lives. Our issues are obstacles to our spirituality.

What meaning can we bring to life?

Life's process is guided by free will. The above suggests that the greater the interest we bring to life or to all the things that make up life, the better our lives will be. Our attitude is a choice and is governed by free will.

> When you know who you are; when your mission is clear and you burn with the inner fire of unbreakable will; no cold can touch your heart; no deluge can dampen your purpose. You know that you are alive.
> — Chief Seattle (American Indian and teacher)

So when someone greets you and says "Hi, what's new?" you can say "Me".

INTROSPECTION

The last introspection was to connect to our Source. This meditation is one of gratitude. For five minutes, feel nothing but gratitude for your place in the Universe.

What did you find: ....
....
....

....
....

Know ThySelf = A passport to happiness

"My Angels whispered messages and led me to the source of Wisdom" – Unknown

Know ThySelf ("Gnothi Seauton" in Greek) is the inscription in the forecourt of the temple of the oracle of Apollo at Delphi.

Delphi is an ancient city in Greece and the site of the famous oracle. Here in the temple of Apollo, the Omphalos (boss on shield) or where the conical stone was believed to mark the centre of the earth. Apollo, the Sun God, was the patron of Truth, and the basic Greek precept was 'Know Thyself.'

Later, Socrates adopted the great dictum 'Know ThySelf', **as surely the first step in every kind of religious enterprise**. (Reference: Classical Greek, CM Bowra, The Everyman's Dictionary of Religion and Philosophy by Geddes Macgregor and Hutchinson Concise Encyclopaedia.)

This book makes the same claim.

The latest research findings at the Delphi site and on the writings of the period, tell us that for several hundred years people travelled from all over the known world to have a reading by one of the practicing oracles. The research does not reveal if the messages given were accurate, but it does indicate the desire of the pilgrims to know more about themselves.

Man who man would be, must rule the empire of himself.
– Percy Bysshe Shelley, 1792 – 1822
(English poet and activist)

When a man's fight begins within himself, he is worth something. – Robert Browning, 1812 – 1889 (English poet)

I thought that I was stupid, when I was merely dyslexic. My belief, coupled with the feeling of not being good enough set up a 'way of being' within myself. It took me many years to unravel my fear and the damage that had been caused. I would not have been successful if I did not know what to unravel. I had to understand the patterns that set off certain behaviours or what resulted from a behavioural type. It was impossible to move forward without really scrutinising every layer that made up my character. I went through and am still going through the process of 'Knowing ThySelf.'

To give insight into what I have learnt about myself would take another book, but one example is to do with the way that I saw myself and how this came about.

Snapshot – Age 4 - Too terrified to speak

When Enid was dating Dad, prior to marrying him, they would pick us up from The German's farm for weekends. Apparently I was so scared that it would take half the weekend to get me to say something. It would seem that I sheltered inside myself and would stay there until I was coaxed out. Perhaps, like a dog that had been beaten too often, I would cower under the table.

When they drove us back I would start to scream in terror. The closer I got to the farm the louder and more frantic I became.

The remembrances that I have were of the man that I call The German. But according to Mum (Enid), it was the wife who was the bad one. I don't remember her and perhaps it is just as well.

When I was in my thirties, in a meditation, I was taken back to the age of a toddler. I remember seeing an argument with Hildegard and Dad. They were fiercely angry with each other and somehow I was hit or knocked over. With that glimpse of the past, I started shaking, at first slowly and then uncontrollably as if I was working a jackhammer. It lasted for about fifty minutes and left me totally drained. Clearly, I was experiencing what I felt at that age.

Mom (Enid) and Dad both worked hard to bring in money to feed, dress and house the six of us. The house was always clean and there was enough food on the table. But, there was not much money left over, and so for large periods of time we only had the basics. This meant that a lot of the time the clothes that I had, had been my older brother John's, and the year before that they had been Keith's. There were long periods of time when nothing new was bought for me and as such I felt second hand. This was a silly thought, as this was not the case. But my mind saw it differently and played inferiority in mind like a stuck record; something like, my clothes are second hand, then so am I. I can assure you that the clothes were fine as Mom would not let her kids run around shabbily dressed.
I did learn though that a lack of money was not a lack of love and the fact that there wasn't much disposable income had no effect on happiness.

As an adult working through my issues:-

I first had to identify the issues. How did any given issue affect my behaviour or emotions? I needed to see when or how it kicked in.
For all of these steps, I needed to seek and find. Understanding the process did not necessarily mean that it was resolved. However, by knowing the patterns, I could modify the resultant behaviours, thereby reducing the effect.

Let me give you another example of the benefit of 'Knowing Thyself.'

Upon ending one relationship, I could not enter into another for a while. I needed time to understand the 'whats' and the 'whys' of that relationship. I did not want to move into another attachment until I had understood what happened in the last one. When a relationship breaks up there is usually confusion and hurt. The hurt comes from things that are said or done by either party. After that break up I had to look at each piece of confusion and make sense of it. In some cases I had to take ownership and responsibility for my behaviour. Yet I had to see clearly enough to know that the (blame) failure of the relationship was not all mine. That way I wouldn't accumulate baggage, nor bring baggage into a new association.

One ex-partner on the other hand immediately went into another relationship. This, I believe, was to hide the 'whats' and 'whys.' She did not want to look too closely because she may have seen that she also contributed to the breakup and was afraid of what she might find. I was able to process the pain. I doubt that she did and it's probably still there buried deep within her. She is likely to experience pain upon pain.

By first looking within and then seeing, and lastly understanding, you are less likely to make the same mistakes. Or, if you do, you will recognise mistakes earlier so as to take responsibility for them.

A top-flight tennis player will research everything he can about an opponent and use the knowledge gained in relation to his *own abilities and weaknesses.* He could not do so if he did not know everything about his own game. The coach of a football team will be aware of every aspect of his team. He will know if his midfield is strong or weak and the backs' ability to defend. He uses this insight to plan each and every match to ensure the best chance of winning. He will use this knowledge to make adjustments within a game.

There is no difference between the sports examples and how you live your life. Knowledge about ThySelf is the key!

Gary Player is rated as one of the top ten golfers of all time. Yet his peers say that Gary had no great ability. If so, then what allowed Gary to win eight majors? What was it in his nature that created so much success? I can't answer these questions. However, I can say with confidence that Gary would have known his strengths and weaknesses and would have worked them accordingly.

Knowing the Different Facets of Yourself

The facets of our character are like boxes. You may have 23 boxes, while I may have 30. There is no fixed number. We are strong in some boxes and weak in others. In some areas of our life we may exude great ability and therefore confidence, in others we may be weak and timid. Our task is to understand each and every box. Where we are strong we must remain strong; where we are weak we must attend to those weaknesses.

In your 23 boxes, 15 may have good positive aspects in them, five could be neutral while the remaining three are negative. But, it could be that the negative three are exerting a massive influence on how you see yourself. Part of your life's purpose is to identify your boxes (Know ThySelf) and strengthen those that are weak. The number of boxes as well as the positive or negative influence will change throughout your life. You will have to scrutinise your boxes constantly.

The topics in this book are likely to represent many of your boxes. Some of the topics may not be your particular boxes. You may have some box types that are not included in this book. It is up to you to know your own boxes.

STOP
Are you who you think you are? Will you be who you think you want to be in the future?

……………………………………………………………………………………………..
……………………………………………………………………………………………..
……………………………………………………………………………………………..
……………………………………………………………………………………………..

INTROSPECTION

You know what is coming don't you? Yes, *your boxes*. Introspect on how many you might have and record them. Remember, you can also have good boxes so look for these as well.

How many boxes did you have? …………………………………………………………..
……………………………………………………………………………………………..
……………………………………………………………………………………………..
……………………………………………………………………………………………..
……………………………………………………………………………………………..

You will need to do this introspection many times and record your finding each time. Then on subsequent introspections, introspect on each separate box. This is a good way to get to know yourself.

There are also times when a strong box becomes weak or a weak one becomes strong, only to become weak again. So it is an ongoing process.

Feeling boxed in? Don't be, the end result is worth it, after all you may just uncover a treasure chest!

Socrates (C 469 - 399 BC, Greek philosopher) says, "Could a man or woman who is knowledgeable about many things be considered wise if they didn't know themselves?"

The more you know about yourself the better you will be at making your life work. For instance, how can you know your wife or husband if you do not know yourself? The more we know about ourselves the more we can discover about others. In fact, as we do not live in a vacuum, we cannot learn about ourselves without learning about others and vice versa.

Do you know yourself? ....
....
....

The answers lie in Knowing ThySelf. This comes about through searching and introspection. You cannot conquer yourself if you do not know yourself.

Your Main Issues

We spoke above about the boxes and how important it is to know and understand these. Within the boxes there are likely to be two or three main issues that will influence your life enormously. They will be woven into the fabric of your relationships, work and home life. We are encouraged to explore these to reduce their effect on our lives. To help in this regard, listen to what people say to you (other people are your mirrors reflecting back at you what you need to know). It is important that you analyse past events in an attempt to see your ongoing patterns. Ask people who know you well what patterns they have observed. Assure them that you will not get angry if they are honest (and don't get angry)! Over a period of time you will gain insight. By understanding trends you will be better able to manage yourself.

It is hard to reach adulthood without some damage. The question is how bad is the damage? When you know what your main life issues are you can take your power back.

Taking Responsibility for Yourself

If you cannot identify your inadequacies, your fears or your limiting beliefs, life will push you around. You need to take responsibility and take the initiative.

From The Buddha: "Though he should conquer a thousand men in the battlefield a thousand times, yet he, indeed, who would conquer himself is the noblest visitor."

When we are born we pass on responsibility for our welfare to others. The same applies when we are old. But what about the middle of your life?

On responsibility and some of the great religions

It is nature's rule, that as we sow, we shall reap.   – Buddhism

Whatever a man sows, that he will also reap and God will render to every man according to his deeds.   – Christianity

"Thou canst not gather what thou dost not sow; as thou dost plant the tree so it will grow"   – Hinduism

---
STOP
So what does taking responsibility really mean to you?

Journal: ....
....
....
....
....

When you approach your so-called problems in life in the manner described, you will have fewer challenges, more friends, better relationships and more money. You won't have to try and hold your head up high - it will be a natural occurrence.

STOP
**When was the last time you took responsibility
for an action that you were not proud of?**

....
....
....

....
....

When I went broke, I owed a lot of money to creditors. It would have been so easy to jump on a plane and leave the country to return to the country of my birth, leaving my debts and worries behind. But I didn't, as I also owed money to family and friends. I could not let them down, irrespective of how uncomfortable it was for me. So by staying to pay my friends back, I could not escape my creditors and also had to pay them. The money that I owed my friends was only about twenty percent of what I owed the creditors, so I ended up paying the entire one hundred percent. I shudder to think what the final amount was as the interest was devastating. It took years to clear and kept me poor for most of that time. But it was worth it as by taking responsibility for the debt, I retained my friends and my integrity.

If you don't take responsibility for your finances, there will be catastrophic consequences. Without taking responsibility for your health, you will over a period of time become sickly. Lack of responsibility in your relationships means, either no relationships or bad relationships. When you do not take responsibility for an issue the opposite of what you want to happen is usually the result.

Let's look at taking responsibility for our health in greater detail. For those people who don't care what rubbish they eat they are likely to say things like, *I eat what I want and what I like.* Imagine the subtle message that they are telling their subconscious. The subconscious will interpret it as *I don't care if I am unhealthy.* So in time, they will become unhealthy.

50/50 in Relationships

Elene Watts, one of the psychologists who worked through this work, told me that research has shown that blame for almost any issue must be taken at least 50% each. This is important to understand because, if you are to take responsibility for yourself, then you need to shoulder your share of the blame. That is, if you're to learn and grow.

Add your thoughts on the above: ....

....

....

....

....

Snapshot – age about twelve – 'A fight with an adult'

Where we grew up there was lots of bush and we used to play Cowboys and Indians. We were rough and at times got hurt. I remember one day John came in with an arrow sticking out of his head! Anyway, there was a time when in a skirmish,

I hit David Bar. I remember his name because we used to call him Baa-Baa as in the nursery rhyme. Being the same age as myself it seemed fair to rough him up a bit - boy he was lucky I didn't scalp him. The next day he came with his Dad and as luck would have it, it was at a time when I was completely on my own. My twelve years of life were no match against a man and so it was not much of a contest. "Fuck with my boy," he said, whilst giving me the first slap on the face. This knocked me to the ground. Every time I got up I was slapped down again and as he did, he snarled at me, "You're a worthless piece of shit."

I was stunned at this brutish behaviour and language from an adult. He did not use a closed fist, as that would have left a mark, but it was gruelling and went on for about twenty minutes. I put up a brave fight, as every time I got up I would assume the correct boxing stance and issue a couple of left jabs in an effort to defend myself. These to him would have been like being brushed with ostrich feathers and so 'cuff', down I would go again. But even so, I'd be damned if I was going to show any fear or respect to him, nor did I apologise for hurting his son. In fact, at the time I wished I had scalped him. Of course this made him madder, which meant the wallops got harder. My old friend - anger - was ever ready and I did my best to beat him up, but what could a twelve-year-old do against a grown man?

Allowing Trust

God does not take you by the hand and say, "Come child, we are going on a rollercoaster ride and when it is finished you will be better off." It is more like you are thrust on the rollercoaster, seemingly on your own. It's frightening and you cannot understand what is happening. Some time during that ride, it is likely you will realise that if you let go and surrender, the ride becomes enjoyable, with all the dips and dives. As you surrender and hand over control, you develop an all-abiding trust. Something far greater than you is in the driving seat and even though you seem to be on your own, you realise that you are not.

By getting in touch with yourself it is easier to let trust flow. When I set out to improve myself and my life, I didn't have any idea what I could achieve, nor who I could become. There was no blueprint or road map. My only hope for a better future lay in trust.

When I gave up working in construction, I gave it up for something more. I did not know what more meant. My future was about as clear as a grimy window. But I went ahead in trust and look how it turned out. As I went along searching, I gained strength of character. This in turn gave me the ability to trust even more. Without trust in myself, the ground I walked on was uneven, rocky and unstable.

I learnt that there are two aspects to trust. The first is that I could trust myself to be creative, to pull through and to prosper. The second is that I learnt to trust in being looked after by Source as in - give us this day our daily bread.

When you can rely on yourself as a result of trusting your ability and that of Source to help you, you will have the confidence to move forward almost unhindered. I say almost unhindered because life is full of challenges. With trust you have the confidence to be able to transcend difficulties.

In this workbook, I have spoken about courage and the claiming of your power. I have given you tools and methods to do this, but if you can learn to trust, then your power and courage will be there for you.

I also speak about fear – fear is a lack of trust, or conversely, when you trust, *there is no* fear. When trust is entered into, fear is erased.

Learn to trust

STOP:
Do you trust that you will be looked after?

Journal: ....
....
....
....
....

Why should we trust in a higher power?

Because there is nothing else in this world that is totally trust worthy.
Rubbish you may say, but hear me out. How many of you have been in a relationship that was great one day and fell apart the next? From that experience you learnt that even the best relationships can go sour.

The same with a job - it is all rosy; until the merger, a new boss or a failing Gross Domestic Product. Now, is your life built on rock or on clay? You appreciate it while it's good, but you can't stake your life on it.

Assume that you are a house - when you are being built you are very cautious that your foundations are deep enough to sit on bedrock. You know that you will sink if you are built on clay or sand. Your relationship may be great and so may your job, but are these the very bedrock that you base your life on? No, must be the answer – how can they be when by nature they are so transient? There is only one bedrock that is totally trustworthy and that is your Source.

You may say, 'Ha, what about me, I can trust myself'. You can't you know. How can you trust yourself, when there are times when you are petulant, angry, unhappy or depressed? We humans go through an array of emotions that we have difficulty controlling. Many times, there is no logical reason for them. Therefore, how on earth can we trust ourselves when we are so unpredictable, so emotional and very often out of balance? We can't, is the answer. We can only trust the bedrock of God.

In life, there are only two constants: one is change, the other is God - it is always there, always supportive.

Describe your bedrock: ....
....
....

There is an old Hebrew saying – Hell is distance from God.

INTROSPECTION

Lower your breathing, relax and focus on trust. Look at it from two aspects, the first not having it and the second what it feels like to have it.

STOP
Why is trust necessary to live an abundant life?

Journal: ....
....
....
....
....

An abundant life is one with enough money to enjoy yourself, good health, happy and mutually rewarding relationships, strong self esteem and of course happiness. Without trust, some of the areas of your life may work, but with trust, all areas of your life will work.

So how do we learn to trust?
Trust comes from several sources. One source is a belief that there is a God, and that God is benevolent. Without a belief in God, whatever you trust will be transient.

The second source comes from accessing your own inner wisdom by going within and letting go of fear and anxiety – without this your life is not likely to improve. Trust is like a mouse, it will not appear if there is any noise - all has to be quiet. For the results of trust to manifest there cannot be one shred of worry. I cannot emphasise this point enough. You will be required to let go of anxiety and sink into a calm mind set. The minute you feel concern coming on, relax your mind and hand over. Then, and only then, will things open up for you.

I believe that fear lowers your vibration. When your vibration is lowered, you attract negativity to yourself.

Do you know that many hobos have great trust? Seems like a contradiction, doesn't it? Generally speaking they are not concerned where their next meal will come from. Perhaps it may not be on time or with silver service, but it will come. It is seldom that beggars die of starvation, they may die of AIDS, or alcohol poisoning, but not starvation. In some respects they have less fear than people with money.

The Pain of Glass (*the ramblings of a writer*)
As I awoke, it was the blood that I remembered. It was from a dream that still cloaked my consciousness.

I was on my own at a travelling fair, absorbed in the moment of swirling rides, colours, laughing children and gay music, when suddenly I was approached by a scruffy man in jeans and a leather jacket. He asked if I would help him carry something heavy.

Even in the dream, I thought of my thin frame and wondered, why me? Nevertheless I followed the man. We went past merry-go-rounds, juggling clowns and food stalls, until we reached a group of people who seemed to be a gang.

He pointed to a man on the ground and, as I looked, I saw that the man was covered in blood. I was told that only 'I' could 'fix' this person. I knelt down and looked more closely. His entire face was a mass of cuts; it looked like a Picasso painting, with cubed glass embedded, as if he had crashed through a window. Around each fragment blood oozed, red and dark. His lips were lacerated, as if a cheese grater had been used on them. This person was in pain, but powerless to remove the glass on his own. Nor could anyone else. I knew it was up to me to help him. I rolled up my sleeves, braced myself and wiggled out the first splinter. He winced, but made no sound.

Then I realised that it was myself on the ground. The person who was led to the body was also me, as it could only be me who could pull the glass splinters out of my face.

(In most of our dreams, we are the main person or object. Dreams, when examined closely, are wonderful tools. They give us valuable information about ourselves).

The worst cuts were around the lips. I was given to understand that the lips represent communication and speaking out, so this was valuable knowledge as the man on the ground had, for most of his life, been powerless at speaking out. I also realised that the size and sharpness of each piece of glass represented the size and sharpness of each hurt.

Slowly and painfully I extracted each piece, or using the analogy, each hurt, until every single fragment had been removed. But it did not end there. Even though the glass had been removed and the immediate pain reduced, there were still scars. Our face is what we present to the world and the wounds were what the world sees, or rather what we think they see. Although I did not see it in the dream, I realised that over time the scars also had to go. They were more than flesh wounds and they represented deeper emotions. The last part of the dream showed my face at my present age, free of scars and healed.

To summarise: We do get hurt, but it is up to us to clear our injuries as nobody else can do this for us. Yes, it can be painful, but if we do not remove them they bite deeper.

Finally, we become stronger as a result of our wounds, but only when we take the time to understand and clear them. If we don't, we remain bleeding and hurt.

STOP
We all carry baggage of some sort. Does the garbage you carry govern your attitude? Or does your attitude govern the baggage you retain?

....
....
....
....

STOP
What do you get out of your dreams?
Do you try to analyse them?
Perhaps start a journal where you write down your dreams.
Try to remember your dreams.

Journal notes: ....
....
....
....

ATTITUDE = forward or backward motion

In our early years of development we may not have been responsible for our attitudes and most of what we thought was bestowed upon us by heredity, environment and school, etc. As thinking adults, we need to form our own opinions and get in touch with our own attitudes and, where necessary, amend them.

We must take responsibility for our perspectives. For instance, you may be stubborn. Stubbornness will impinge on relationships but it can also be a good trait in as much it may give you staying power. It could be one of a dozen attributes that you have unconsciously been allowing to rule your life. By knowing that aspect of yourself, you can be aware of when you are being stubborn and take responsibility for it.

Make the most of yourself, for that is all there is of you.
- *Ralph Waldo Emerson, 1803 – 1882,*
(U.S. philosopher and essayist)

STOP
Do you make the most of yourself?

Journal notes: ....

....

....

....

....

....

Becoming

If you use your wisdom, you will become wiser, as wisdom grows wisdom. If you feel love, you will receive love as giving love grows love. If you are in happiness, it will create more happiness and so on.

Ignorance = Disempowerment

If you analyse the word ignorance - ignore means a refusal to take notice. Put another way, ignorance is not taking responsibility. Of course within the context of this book, we refer to the taking of responsibility for our own issues.

Whoever said, 'Ignorance is bliss', was truly ignorant. The benefits of knowledge or of applied knowledge (wisdom) are untold. Only a fool and an ostrich would bury his head in the sand.

Ignorance is denial. It is denial of the universal law of cause and effect. Astuteness is better but necessitates taking responsibility.

Ignorance is an indulgence. It is finding distractions so real issues don't have to be broached.

Ignorance can come out of fear. The attitude is, 'rather the devil I know, than the one I don't.' See the truth about yourself and 'the truth shall set you free.'

Once again, you need to be conscious of your thoughts, to be aware of what is happening in you head.

The opposite of ignorance is wisdom, but wisdom only serves us if it offers a solution to a problem.

Knowing ThySelf and Action (awareness)

The action required to know yourself is awareness. This sounds easy but in practice it's not. We tend to get swallowed up by issues. If you can, stand back and take the time to see all the components, to be aware of your attitudes, why you think about certain issues as you do. Although it is good to analyse after the event, it is better to have the awareness while it is happening. With practice it gets easier.

The teachings of Buddha say, "If a king was plagued by bandits, he must know where those bandits are camped so that he can destroy them."

> **STOP**
> **Think again and be honest; how often do you let yourself feel down?**
> **Trends in your journal should show you**
> **the ups and downs of your mindset.**

Trends: ....
....
....

Self observation is such a delightful and extraordinary thing. After a while you don't have to make any effort, because as illusions begin to crumble, you begin to know things that cannot be described.   - De Mellow (Author of Awareness)

Knowing ThySelf and Your Scripts

Scripts are modes of behaviour that are sometimes good, sometimes bad. They are normally developed in our first few years of life and are recurring patterns of behaviour. Although we need to understand our good scripts, for this discussion we will only concern ourselves with the negative scripts. Some examples:

We have all heard of women who go from a relationship where they were *physically abused,* only to find themselves in another where they are also treated in much the same way. This is likely to be a recurring negative script. There are people who can't hold down a job, because they are so negative about their own self-worth. This is also a front.

The following is a script about myself: For many years, I felt that I had forgiven The German. As an adult I had no resentment. Yet it was only in my 45th year that I realised that I was still living in the script that I had created between 18 and 36 months-of-age. The script became a template for my life and ruled me on many issues.

We all have recurring issues (scripts). If we look closely at ourselves and reflect (introspect) on our past, we invariably see recurring patterns. By Knowing ThySelf, we can address these and try and break the cycle. Once we understand and accept that these exist, we start to grow.

Examples of scripts are: I am not good enough. I feel guilty if I have a good time. People don't like me.

STOP
Spend some time identifying your main scripts. Look for both good and bad. Then note how they have affected your life.

What are your scripts? ....
....
....
....
....

For more on scripts, see Eric Berne's 'Script Analysis'. It is an amazing book.

A script that I set up within my self was that I detested anything that smacked of authority. Remember when you read my story, My Brother John, and some other writings about the German man? Well, I think that my aversion to authority was developed through his controlling behaviour. I rebelled, and still do, against the army in Australia (who tried to conscript me), teachers, anything to do with the Government, big business, and I detest the control that banks have over us. All have felt my wrath. For most of my working life I have worked for myself, so there was no control over me. By allowing myself to be affected as I have been, I had given my energy away. Whereas I should have just let it go.

Some people may refer to scripts as 'the inner child' issues. There are many books on the inner child. I suggest that you read some of them. You need to know yourself and why you act in certain ways or respond the way you do when you are fed specific stimuli. Without understanding this you will not gain any mastery over yourself.

Knowing ThySelf by Articulation

Jumbled thoughts or concepts come to mind on a regular basis, especially when you open your mind to exploration. More often than not, they remain just that - jumbled thoughts. It is only when you are able to articulate them either verbally or by writing them down that you can decipher and understand these thoughts in a cohesive format. That is why it is so important that you use a journal.

When we articulate thoughts, we can convey them clearly to other people. They may agree or disagree. Either way, it can stimulate debate. Debate will expand our store of knowledge even further. For instance, allowing others to challenge our beliefs will accelerate your growth. Always make sure you listen to other points of view, and then form your own opinions. Perhaps think about these in your sessions of introspection.

STOP
Think about a time today when perhaps you were driving, or waiting for someone. Try and remember what you thought about. The chances are that your thoughts were jumbled.

Thoughts……………………………………………………………………………………..
………………………………………………………………………………………………..
………………………………………………………………………………………………..
………………………………………………………………………………………………..
………………………………………………………………………………………………..

Knowing ThySelf and Teaching

As a result of learning about yourself you will become wiser. It is impossible to learn about yourself and not learn about other people. Automatically as you gain more insights, you will also become a teacher. You will find that people will gravitate towards you, like a moth to a flame. It is wonderful when this happens for there is no greater task than to help others. Whether you become a good teacher will depend on your sincerity, empathy and compassion

By teaching you will increase your knowledge and wisdom - as we teach what we need to learn.

About 15 years ago I did a course called 'The Forum'. It was a wonderful course and helped me tremendously. At the end, as a sort of passing out parade, we all had to coin a phrase that meant something important to each of us. We were to tell the audience what this was. At the time I didn't know where mine came from, but subsequently it has proven to be accurate. I said,' *I empower myself so as to empower others'*.

Knowing ThySelf and Remembering

Everyday, we learn something about ourselves. Normally, we forget and it passes us by. Thoughts and understanding are vague and fleeting. You want your ideas to remain a permanent part of yourself. By writing them down you impress them on your mind. By recording your inspirations you add to your store of knowledge about yourself. By going back you reinforce what you know and hopefully become a better person as a result. For me this is not drudgery, it inspires me.

Those who cannot remember the past are condemned to repeat it.

– George Santayana

Knowing What Thy Want To Be = Forward motion

Have you thought about who you want to be? If not, then you are likely to fall short of your potential. Once you have a better idea of 'who you are', it makes sense to identify who you want to be in the future. You might find that you are happy with the current you. You may determine that you only need tweaking or maybe a quantum leap is required.

By knowing who you want to be, you can determine your personal goals. You will be able to ascertain your values and moral code. You will know where the grey areas are and what is acceptable. This knowledge will govern your relationships and commitments to family, friends and business associates. When you have set values, it removes the anxiety from making decisions, which could create conflict. Time and emotion is not wasted as your personal standards rule.

An understanding of who you want to be will take time and thought. The fact that you are doing this workbook will help in the formulation of the guiding principles for your life.

> **STOP**
> A wonderful method to help clarify who you want to be is
> an introspection that places you on your deathbed.
> From that position, think of what you would have been proud
> of achieving and what you may have been uncomfortable with.
> Consider the eulogy at your funeral or the memory that
> your family and colleagues will have of you.

....
....
....

EGO = A trigger of our actions and behaviour

When in ego, you will only hear your own argument. It is your ego that will keep you in a state of anger, depression or resentment for longer than necessary. It will hinder you from apologising or admitting that you were wrong. Your ego will distance your mind from the present moment while in conversation and will prejudge and filter people out. It will ensure that you tell people how clever you are or how stupid they are (which is the same as saying how clever you are) and even dictate how you conduct yourself in an argument.

> **STOP**
> Re-read the above and see if any of it fits your
> circumstances. Write the answer in your journal.

....
....
....

Justifying the Ego

The ego consumes an immense amount of energy, money and time to uphold its importance. It is wonderful at manipulating the truth by thinking things like; it's all about status symbols. I need to drive X car for my position or I have to wear that label. We are great at hiding the truth from ourselves. In fact, there is nothing wrong with driving an expensive car, wearing exclusive clothes or having a great tan. Be true to yourself by knowing what is really going on. Be aware, we live in a world where we are ruled by illusions. The ego is the creator of illusions.

> **STOP**
> **Introspect on the illusions that you have.**
> **Is your position an illusion?**
> **What about the image you want from the car that you drive?**

....
....
....

How do you see yourself? Example: If you are an accountant, you may have an image (illusion) of being conservative and meticulous.

Record your thoughts: ....
....
....
....
....

INTROSPECTION

Strip away all the illusions that cloak you, that rule your mind. If you can do this you will get as close to your soul as a human can.

Journal notes: ....
....
....
....
....

The ego is nothing more than a set of thoughts that define you. It is your perception of who you are and how you should interact with the world around you. These perceptions seem real and are forceful, normally to your detriment. If you can understand that the ego is nothing more than your perceptions then you can govern it in a way that is healthier for you.

Ego and Survival

Nevertheless, without your ego your survival tools would be diminished. It is self-centredness or self love if you will, that ensures your survival. By looking out for yourself, you are able to avoid threatening situations. Author and teacher Sue Prescott says, "The ego influences you through your emotions to take care of yourself". And De Mello wrote, "To me, selfishness seems to come out of an instinct for self-preservation which is our deepest and first instinct". The ego, if not controlled, can be a drain and a burden. You need to be aware when it makes its presence felt. You can pick up the signals when the ego wants to over-impose itself. You will only know the effect your ego has on you by observation.

A Framework for Describing the Ego

The Concise Oxford Dictionary defines 'conscious' as: aware, knowing, state of being, totality of a person. It is a separation of the spiritual self. It defines the ego as 'the conscious thinking subject' and egocentric as 'centred in the ego'. It includes terms such as self-centred, egotistical, self-interested, self-opinionated. All of these are the spiritual opposite of you. We are not the ego. The ego is an overlay, invariably of fear, negativity, selfishness, etc. It is synonymous with our personality, which is usually formed in early childhood. Strip away the ego and we get the higher self. The ego is the part of you that is transient and dies when the body experiences physical death.

The ego line

Ego can be represented as given below:

Higher Self _____ Extreme Ego

We need to try and move away from the extreme right and towards the centre where we can have balance.

Snapshot – Me

To give you an idea of how to evaluate the ego line, I use myself as an example: Most of my life was spent sitting on the right of the ego line. My anger kept me there as did my lack of self-esteem. When I felt those hateful thoughts at Old Man Baa Baa as he beat me up, I was as far right as anyone could go. Boozing and the resentment kept me there. Being the bully that I was, as well as all my negativity, bolted me to the spot. I was there so often it felt like home.

As I worked on myself and became more in tune with the Universe, I was able to remove the bolts.

Understanding the dynamics of the line made it easier for me to move towards the left and as I did, it was then that my life started to work. I became happier, had less anger and my self-esteem improved. Even so, from time to time I still get pulled back to the right. But because I understand how much better it is towards the left, it is easier to move away from the extreme right. There are times when I feel the bliss of a visit to the far left (I have never been all the way to the left), but most of the time I fluctuate between twenty points to the left and twenty to the right of centre. That position is a fairly good one, as the next section will show.

We are human

The majority of people gravitate to the right of the ego line; this is not unnatural. Just don't live there. To retain balance you must venture to the left as often as possible. When you move to the left, you are experiencing the Divinity within. As we become wiser and more spiritual it becomes easier to spend more time towards the left as emotions arising from being in the right are reduced.

When we spend time in the extreme right we tend to lose ourselves, become stressed and unreasonable. If you walk in the mountains or come out of your church, temple or ashram you are likely to be more to the left. When you have just made love to someone you love, or have kissed your sleeping child, then you are likely to be closer to the left.

This is the entire point of life, to be human (ego) but at the same time know your Higher Self. For some it may be a challenge but with determination, positive results can be achieved. You will learn that you do not have to spend all your time in the Ego (right) and you don't have to languish there.

The ego line as given above is a construct or a method to give you a conceptual framework that will allow you to be able to visualise the ego versus the God/Love dynamic. But it is not really a line, as that would indicate that there is distance or space between God and ourselves. This would be incorrect as there is no distance or space between us.

STOP
Sit quietly and contemplate where your ego forms or rules
your personality and what illusions you live with.
Record your perceptions in your journal.

INTROSPECTION

In your introspection today, look at the day thus far and plot where you think you spent most of your time along the ego line. It is a good idea to do this as often as possible. Record the results.

Journal notes: ....

....

....
....
....

The following is a list of 'Ego' words which can be found on the right of the ego line:

Defensiveness, hatred, negativity, selfishness, aggression, miffed, conceit, demanding, fear, temper, abusive, irritability, judgmental, vanity, arrogance, critical, insecurity, huff.

If you have been told, more than once, that you are any of the above then it is likely that you need to work on ego issues. If more than three words consistently represent your state of mind, watch out!

When you move to the left, the issues that these words represent fall away.

STOP
Do any of the above words apply to you?
If so, which words do you think you need to remove?

Journal notes: ....
....
....
....
....

Ego and fear

Ego does a wonderful job of covering up fear. For instance, it will hide an inadequate attitude by suggesting to you that everybody or everything is out to get you.

Ego and Personality

Although it's detrimental to live permanently to the right of the ego line, we need to understand that as humans we have a persona or personality. Our personality is formed through our ego and is what makes me different from you and each of us different from everyone else.

There is no escaping personality, nor would we want to, just don't get lost in it. Don't let it define you and be aware that it is the personality that places the illusions squarely on your shoulders.

Journal: ....
....
....
....

The Higher Self and Ego

There may have been times when you were confused about something and became inefficient as a result. Something may have prompted you to sit down and think it through. By doing so you probably gained clarity and an understanding that took away the confusion. It is that clarity that comes from your Higher Self. When you were lost in the confusion, you were in your ego. When you considered the issues, you moved towards your Higher Self and your Higher Self gave you the answers.

You know the story of Snow White and The Seven Dwarfs. Let's analyse the story from the point of view of understanding the Higher Self versus Ego/Personality issues.

Snow White represents all the Higher Self aspects such as happiness, love, thoughtfulness, contentment, compassion and goodness. In fact, white signifies purity. Sounds boring doesn't she?

On the other hand, the wicked witch (or is it mother-in-law?) is full of her own issues (ego). She is consumed with the desire to be the *loveliest in all the land*. Is being the loveliest in the land relevant? Is this not illusion? Her need to uphold this self-image drove her to want to commit murder. Her entire personality was compromised, generating wicked and evil thoughts. What insecurities did she have that made her so dark? Why, for instance, when she looked into the mirror did she not see other worthwhile attributes. I know on occasions, we get carried away by our insecurities, but she became so caught up in her emotions that she was prepared to kill for them!

Fortunately, most of us are not like that old hag and certainly we are not like the wimpish Snow White. The analogy is indicative of the Higher Self versus ego issues and how we get caught up in issues of the mind. We need to learn to move through illusion to being grounded and we can only do this when we look closely at ourselves and take responsibility. Imagine giving the "old bat" a copy of Know ThySelf?

STOP
Have you ever been the wicked witch?

....
....

....
....

Mum

Enid, the wonderful person who became my mother, is one of those rare people who is totally without ego. Throughout her entire life she has been able to live in the freedom of not needing to strut or boast in any way. She was equally as comfortable as a drama teacher at some of the finest girls' schools in Sydney, or a barmaid. She has been both. Mum recently turned eighty-two and for a present, one of her painter friends offered to paint her portrait. When it was finished Mum was thrilled with the result. The artist's truth came out in the work and portrayed mom as she is – old. Everything on her face looked tired and worn. There were lumps, bumps and drooping bits. Blood vessels showed, as did her wrinkles, while canyons criss-crossed her old face. She is proud of her worn face and delighted to see the resemblance to her past relatives - relatives as she had seen them when she was young and they were old.

Her attitude is the opposite to most of us, who want to be made younger, slimmer more muscular. We are never satisfied with who we are and want to be something bigger or better.
I bless her for what she taught me.

STOP
Re read the above. What resonates with you?

....
....
....
....

Ego and Responsibility

To be happy and well-adjusted, in a life that works, requires balance. Too much time spent on the left (spiritual) without solving the problems on the right (via lessons and clearing issues) means that you will not learn life's lessons. You will not progress and life is likely to gang up on you.

Your ego can keep you in a place of fear, thereby limiting your potential.

> **STOP**
> Identify how your ego can stifle your ability to function. If you are short of material, browse through your journal and I'm sure you will pick a topic fairly quickly.

Journal: ....
....
....
....
....

Ego – (The ramblings of a writer)

Ego, why are you so big and push to emerge at every opportunity? Do you have to shout to be heard over everyone else? Each new meeting is an opening for you to be noticed. Why? Is your importance so great that you must detract from every encounter? Why can't you be quiet so I can concentrate on the person in front of me? But like a demanding child, you pop up irrespective of the relevance to the conversation, screaming for attention without a care for others. Why?

By taking the stage, are you more likely to impress? What impresses are actions and example. Not the loud, 'I am this' or 'I am that!' And Ego, did you know that people don't usually care who you are or what you have done? Their own ego is running their show.

I realise sadly that even though I have had contact with thousands of people, no one really knows me. I tell them what I want them to know, slanting the picture and hiding things that I don't want them to see in me - all because of you my Ego.

How many people really know you? ....
....
....
....
....
....
....

Lastly, on Ego: "No matter how rich you become, how famous or powerful, when you die the size of your funeral will still pretty much depend on the weather."
— Michael Pritchard

YOUR JOURNAL

By now your journal should be starting to fill up with all sorts of interesting things about yourself. For today, put down Know ThySelf and read your journal. Look for trends and insights.

Journal: ………………………………………………………………………………..

………………………………………………………………………………………………

………………………………………………………………………………………………

………………………………………………………………………………………………

………………………………………………………………………………………………

………………………………………………………………………………………………

………………………………………………………………………………………………

Illusions

What are they? 'A Course in Miracles' says, 'If God didn't make it, then it does not exist'. Whew, that's strong. What does that mean about all the issues that fill your mind? Did God make them?

Suppose you are a sales person and at the start of the year you set goals to achieve X quantity of sales. But after three months you receive your sales report and your sales are well below what you had targeted. This news depresses you and you go home in a negative state.

But, what really happened? You set targets and you had a couple of bad months. Motivated yesterday and disillusioned today. Where did the depression come from? Nothing has changed, except your happiness. The depression came from stuff in your mind that said to you, *you are not good enough; you can never achieve your targets*. These thoughts are illusions.

Another example of illusions is status. Do we really need status?

Then there is the thought that you will be happy if you get married, or that life will be horrible if you get divorced. There is a saying that marriage is like a town under siege – those that are in the town want out, and those that are out want in. In both cases, illusion rules. Our entire life is filled with illusions, that is, thoughts that are not real, thoughts that serve no purpose. If there is one thing that you get from this work, I hope that it is an understanding of the waste, the silliness and the futility of carrying illusions in your mind.

My Concise Oxford Dictionary describes an illusion as 'deception, delusion; sensuous perception of an external object involving a false belief'. So all of those thoughts that just clutter our minds have no basis and are transitory.

Your day dreams are illusions, unless you have the strength of character to turn them into reality.

Photographs and Memories

'Who are you?' crooned the caterpillar.
Alice replied rather shyly, 'I – I hardly know. I knew who I was when I got up this morning, but I think I must have changed several times since then.'
                                                    - Lewis Carroll

What is your core? Is it an illusion? Is it a constellation of a million personalities, or facets of a thousand inconsistent moods?

Some find their persona in their work and say, 'I am an accountant' and expect you to feel their importance or 'I am an academic' and show you this by carrying a sheaf of impressive-looking papers under a bent arm. Are you your work?

So who are you? Are you your memories and photos?

....
....
....
....

STOP
Someone once said, when referring to their past life, that "It was like a dream." My comment is, could it have been an illusion? If you don't have photos, memories or possessions, how would you see your past life? It would have to be like a dream or illusion. The only thing that may make it real for you would be the *emotion* that you retain of all your life events. So if you are the sum total of your emotions, what is the illusion now?

What are your thoughts on this?

....
....
....
....

INTROSPECTION

How do we become aware of the illusions that fill our minds?
Make yourself comfortable and close your eyes. Tell your mind to be blank for five minutes and then push all thoughts from your mind. You may do this successfully for 15 to 20 seconds. But then an intrusive thought may cross your mind. You may pick this up quickly, or it may hijack your mind and take you on a merry song and dance. But then you finally realise that there is an intrusion, wipe the slate of your mind clear (again) and re-focus. However, some seconds later, the process may be repeated.

What you have learnt is that even when trying to keep a clear mind, it is very difficult. You learnt that the mind has a 'mind of its own' and introduces what it wants. This happens all day, everyday. The only time we have a semblance of control, is when we are concentrating on something, such as when we are at our desk writing a document. But get up from the desk to go and get coffee and the mind reclaims control. Before we know it we are thinking about something it wants to think about.

These intrusions are illusions. With each unsolicited thought, we are taken away from reality into dream. Yet, our minds will have it that, if we take away the dreams, we move into the unknown.

STOP
Go into an introspection and see yourself living a life
of reality, of mind purity, of no illusion.
Most people panic when they are first confronted
with this thought. They get scared that they will lose control.
But it is through the stripping of the illusions
that real control emerges, as does the peace.

Journal: ....
....
....
....

You will have dreams, but fight for clarity, understand that you are not the billions of unsolicited thoughts.

Another way of looking at the above; what if I gave you a choice, that by the wave of a magic wand, you would not ever get lost in negative thoughts again. But would you accept, as by doing so, you would strip yourself of your carefully constructed persona.

Imagine, just for a moment, if all of mankind removed their illusions, just how different we would be. There would be just love. Fear would be unheard of. Nor would there be jealousy or hate. There would be abundance, and all would be harmony – just as it was meant to be.

But not only that, many industries would collapse. For instance, with no illusions and a balanced perspective, hair growth companies would have reduced sales. The same would apply to hair removal and slimming products or treatments. Steroids are likely to fall away as there would be less people needing to express who they are through big muscles. As the advertising industry failed at appealing to our self esteem deficiencies, it would have to focus elsewhere.

Journal: ………………………………………………………………………………………..
………………………………………………………………………………………………….
………………………………………………………………………………………………….
………………………………………………………………………………………………….
………………………………………………………………………………………………….

ACCEPTANCE = Tranquillity

Do you get depressed? Lots of people do. Some people are diagnosed with chemical imbalances in the brain, which supposedly cause depression. Most however, get depressed as a result of negativity. This is because things in life may not be going as smoothly as they could be. The mind takes over and after thousands of, *'It is just too difficult'* or *'Why did this happen to me?'* they get depressed. This might last for a couple of hours, several days or even years. A state of depression in most cases is an extreme case of negativity.

STOP
Do you ever get depressed?
Do you feel down on a fairly regular basis?
Can you see that most depression is just a bad case of negativity?

Do you get depressed? ....
....
....
....
....

INTROSPECTION

Try and take yourself into a depression. That's right - get depressed. Then you will remember what that feeling is like. The best way to do this is to reconnect with a time when you were depressed. It is only by becoming familiar with the feeling of depression that you will be able to recognise it when it materialises and thereby be able to dismantle it. Can you see how easy it is to create depression with your thoughts? Before coming out of this introspection, imagine yourself feeling great.

Journal: ....
....
....
....
....

A key to tranquillity

One of the keys to a workable life is acceptance – acceptance of yourself, your past and your current situation. Life is likely to be difficult if you are inflexible. Therefore it requires tolerance. There will always be situations or people in your life that do not suit you. Accept them for who or what they are. Acceptance is important if you want to be calm.

A Yiddish proverb says: "If all pulled in one direction, the world would keel over."

Elsewhere in this book I have talked about polarity: light and dark, hot and cold, love and hate, etc. Our planet has this diversity. Within this diversity there are many lessons to learn. One of the greatest is acceptance. We have different cultures, skin colours, languages.

> **STOP**
> **Consider what you think are your imperfections.**

....
....
....
....

An Intellectual Acceptance

Agreeing or disagreeing with, for example, a political issue, is a form of acceptance. You will come to a conclusion or an understanding as a result of a linear thought process. These are not the types of acceptance issues that I refer to. I'm talking about situations with an emotional content – generalisations, prejudice, etc. It is the uncomfortable issues that we need help with, those circumstances or people where there are emotional attachments.

> **STOP**
> **Look for a time when you were in a situation where you did not let go. Identify why you did not let go. Can you see how you would have been better off had you reached a point of acceptance?**

Journal: ....
....
....
....
....
....

Acceptance of Yourself

This entire book is about you and how you view yourself. It is not how you see yourself that creates limitations in your mind. It is how you see yourself in relation to others. For instance, if you were the only person on the planet, would it matter if you had a tennis ball sized wart on the end of your nose? No, it wouldn't. But now see yourself as part of humanity and you are likely to be self conscious about it. Once again, it is not the wart that is the issue. It is your thought process about how you think others view you that suggests that you are a freak.

Here is a contradiction: Nobody is perfect; we all have defects. Yet in our imperfection we are perfect.
Record what you consider are your imperfections: ....
....
....
....
....
....
....
....

Accept these imperfections as a part of who you are. They are unique signatures separating you from everyone else. I for instance have the largest eyebrows in the world. They are so large that I have to cut them. Yes, I know men are not supposed to cut their eyebrows but if I don't I can't see. I feel like a sheep dog peering through a hedge and have been called 'eyebrow challenged'. It has been suggested that I have big fat slugs lying across the top third of my head. I have a friend, Paul, who says that my eyebrows remind him of the hedgerows from his native England. He also postulates that like hedgerows - there could be all sorts of creatures, big and small living there.

Seriously though, we should see our imperfections as an aspect of who we are, as part of our uniqueness. So I get on with it by getting out the chain saw once a month and trimming down the overgrowth and then forgetting all about my eyebrows.

STOP
Using those deficiencies that you identified about yourself, take each one in turn and make a funny or endearing comment about it. See them as part of yourself, your special signature. Have the same compassion for yourself as you would for your child, should your child have a 'supposed' deficiency.

Journal: ....
....
....
....
....
....

....
....

If your difference is one of a disabling nature, you have to remain positive in spite of it. A wonderful Edgar Allen Poe story I read about forty years ago had a profound effect on me. It was a short story called, 'The Valley of the Blind'. Essentially it was about a tribe in South America who had a genetic flaw, which rendered the members of the tribe sightless. As a result of being blind, their other senses evolved. Members of the tribe who were able to see, were considered disabled as they viewed sight as a limitation.

Recently I overheard a conversation about statistics emerging from a research project. It seems that where 98% of people tested did not fully accept themselves. It showed that their perceived inadequacies limited their potential to a major degree. The percentages from this research project may or may not be accurate. However, there is likely to be credibility in the findings. Most people do not see their beauty, only their limitations and, as such, limit themselves.

STOP
Ask yourself if have you ever wanted to be someone else?
What about a film star or someone in the public eye?
If so, why? Could the reason be that you
assume that you would escape your issues?

Journal: ....
....
....
....
....
....

Acceptance of Others

We are all different, yet the same. We are powerful but weak, smart and sometimes dumb. We glow with beauty and other times we project gloom. We are all one and should be all 'for' one. You may not rejoice in all the differences but do not judge the differences because judgement (as you will learn later) has an emotional attachment.

Acceptance of others does not mean you have to like everybody. It is just acceptance. It is allowing someone to be different from you. If you don't feel comfortable around a person, then move away.

Acceptance is Patience
There are times when you want a situation to immediately change. Accept with patience the ebb and flow of life. When you accept a situation, you do not have to accept second best. Acceptance is more of an acknowledgement of the status quo. With acknowledgement comes responsibility for the part that you have played in the creation of the situation and a challenge to generate something better.

What is accepted today may not have been accepted yesterday
It is a good idea to remain open-minded when it comes to what we term morals and ethics, because they change with the times and from culture to culture.

You can only move out of a situation once you accept It
If you find yourself in an unwanted situation, the first step is to accept it. Without acceptance, you will be unable to distance yourself from it. If you do not accept the situation, it could possibly break you. You may get out of that issue but you will repeatedly find yourself back in a similar situation until you accept it for what it is and move away from it.

Acceptance and Happiness
You cannot be in a situation that you don't accept and be happy. If you allow the situation to negate your happiness you are a prisoner of your own thoughts. It is better to accept the situation for what it is and do the best you can to change or get out of it. But remain positive and happy. Remember, we do not find happiness, we are happiness. It is within us.

Have you ever heard phrases like the following, *"If I marry her, she will make me happy"*. Does that mean if you do not marry that person you can't be happy?

INTROSPECTION

When composed, I want you to accept your life or rather the difficulties in your life. When you are composed, search your mind for difficulties and relax into them. Don't leave the introspection until you feel more relaxed about those difficult situations.

Jot down in your journal what you learned ………………………………………….

....
....
....
....
....

LOVE OR FEAR

In the section on emotions (below) you will learn that emotions are either love or fear-based. All the above ego words are fear-based, i.e. to the right of the ego line. Love-based emotions are left.

Emotions/Feelings = drivers of behaviour

We cannot live without emotions, nor would we want to as emotions and feelings reveal things about ourselves. That is, provided we listen.

We talk a lot about fear and in some ways it is hard to avoid as it is all around us. For instance, how do most insurance companies market their policies? They do it by putting fear into you – they urge you to imagine what would happen if your house burns down, or your roof has a leak and damages all your furniture, or if you have a car accident, etc. The same applies to medical aid companies - what if you have cancer or a heart attack? Security companies do it by telling you, 'This alarm may stop you from being robbed or raped'. This is their message, but it is how you take them on that is important. Do they affect you and do they get added to your already large fear structure?

Fear is not normally for right now – it is fear of the future

Snapshot – age ten - Anger

With all the anger that resided in me, I became a bully in my own right. I picked on kids, persecuted them and bashed them all over the place. One time it was with a brick, another time I punched a boy (Trevor) in the stomach. He was so bruised he had to take three days off school. I tied one poor kid to a tree down the bottom corner of the school. This was at morning recess and I left him there until lunchtime.

Later on, I even picked a fight with a teacher. This wasn't very bright as he was a physical education teacher and was well-muscled. Man- o- man, I should have picked on the wimpish music teacher. I had so much tension in me that I did not know when I would explode. But I was really lucky to pick that physical education teacher as he was wonderful. He calmed me down without negating my self worth, he didn't become angry, nor did he report me to the headmaster.

As I got older and left school, the fighting continued. In those years I must have had at least twenty brawls in pubs. I only had my last fight at about twenty-seven. Even so, for years after it didn't take much for my anger to erupt.

The only way to understand our emotions is by listening and observing them when they manifest.

Essentially, emotions are an agitation of the mind. Some people are more inclined to have these emotions than others. Words that describe negative emotions are: jealousy, anger, hate, frustration, sadness. Whenever these emotions appear, our behaviour tends to become irrational.

I learnt that anger is an absence of balance.

Feelings are either love or fear- based. Jealousy, envy and anger are fear-based. Compassion, understanding and happiness are love-based.

STOP
On which end of the EGO line would the words *jealousy*,
***envy* or *anger* reside?**

Do you hold any of these? ....
....
....
....
....

Think back on your day. Have you used any fear based words? ....
....
....
....

What emotions did you experience? Were they good or bad emotions? Were they fear- or love-based? ....
....
....
....

Lastly, why did you have those feelings? ....
....
....
....

A test for anger

George, a kinesiologist, taught me some thirty years ago about the weakening affect of anger (or any other negative thought process) on the body. He had me stand facing me, with one arm extended at right angles to my body.
Standing in front of me, he started to push my extended arm down towards the floor. As he did, I was to resist. He could feel the resistance.

Then he had me think hate thoughts. Then, when pushing down the extended arm, there was absolutely no resistance. When I thought loving thoughts the resistance returned.

I suggest that you get a partner to test this process. What it proves is that our physical body is weakened when in a negative condition. Of course, a weakened body will not have the energy required to metabolise food, or to regenerate cells. Therefore if you are in a negative state for long periods, you risk serious illness.

Emotions are Tools for Growth

All emotions, if understood, are tools for growth. We have to have experienced negative emotions to understand the positive. But just experiencing the negative is not enough. We need to consciously embrace the positive. For instance, **'The absence of sadness does not mean we are happy'**. Or the **absence of anger does not mean we are calm**. Even if we are not sad, we must still seek happiness. When we are not angry, we must still look for calm. By remembering sadness we can be happier, by knowing the anger, we can reach greater levels of tranquillity. It is a proactive approach.

> **STOP**
> **Have you felt that at times you may not have been sad, but happiness was lacking? Or were there times when you were not angry, but were not tranquil?**
> **Write the answer in your journal.**

Journal: ....
....

....
....
....
....
....

We cannot banish emotions, but when we understand them we are more able to rein them in.

Emotions and Fear

"There is no evil in the world that you cannot trace to fear" Fear is the strongest emotion, other than love and has the greatest effect on your emotional state. — De Mellow

Eric Clapton sings, "We get lost in our fears".

> **STOP**
> **Have you ever been lost in your fears?**

Journal notes: ....
....
....
....
....

The fear I refer to is not the type that you would experience in a life-threatening event. It is fear gained from an accumulation of many issues over time.

Fear, if left uncontrolled, is sinister in the extreme. It sneaks up on you in the most insidious ways and has you in a debilitating grip (depression) before you know it. Yet it can be defeated. You can remove it with awareness and attention, being in the *present moment* and focusing upon it. When your attention is drawn to dissolving the feeling, like a coward it withers and disappears.

When you are in the clutches of fear, you are not in the **present moment.** This could result in panic, knots in your stomach, sweaty palms and a racing heart. Adrenaline will flood your system, causing many other symptoms. When you are in this state, you cannot function properly. Your thoughts will be scattered and concentration will be difficult. Maybe you are imagining the consequences of your electricity bill not being paid, your boss shouting at you or your boyfriend eyeing your best friend.

STOP
Look and understand the feeling that causes the knots
in your stomach, or your racing heart.

Journal notes: ………………………………………………………………………………..
………………………………………………………………………………………………….
………………………………………………………………………………………………….
………………………………………………………………………………………………….
………………………………………………………………………………………………….

When you focus as suggested above, the feeling will go. Really it will, at least for the time being. Your negativity will be replaced with a more positive mindset, allowing you to take control and function again. You do not have to be at home in the quiet of your bedroom to do this focus. You can do it at work, on the bus or even driving. You will learn that, over a period of time, the fear will return less and less often. The bible says, **"Perfect love casts out fear"** (1Jo 4:18)

You Create your Own Emotions

Feelings or emotions don't just appear, you build them in the factory of your mind. Some people would say that emotions are just chemical reactions. You can release the chemicals.

Emotions are natural but it is how you respond to emotions that is important. When you understand that they are natural to humans and that you will always have them, it helps to understand that you are not weak or silly for having them.

When you know that emotions are a natural part of life, you can take heart. But you still have to be responsible for your emotions.

How to clear destructive emotions

Emotions left to run riot are destructive. You cannot control emotions by force of will, but you can replace them with something better. The most important thing is to identify that you are in the grip of negative emotions. Once you have done this, you switch your focus to something positive.

Long term emotions

When you practice the teachings of this work and improve your confidence and self-worth (when you have a stronger connection to the Creator), when you are more love- than fear-based, then you will find that many of the negative emotions that have gripped you for so long will fall away.

STOP
Think of a time when you 'created' your own emotional state.
Write the answer in your journal.

Journal: ....
....
....
....
....

Taking Responsibility

De Mello teaches that there are four steps to wisdom:

1. Get in touch with your negative feelings.

2. Understand that the feelings you have are not real, even though they seem real.

3. Never identify with the feeling. That is, if you are feeling guilty don't let this become a part of who you are.

4. Wake up and release it. (This last point is brutal, but it is what I have been saying throughout this book – that until you understand it, you cannot release it)

Feelings, such as being sad or guilty, are not necessarily bad. They are only detrimental if you allow them to continue for long periods of time, and so it depends on how long you choose to wallow in them. The longer, the more detrimental their effect. There is a choice – you can languish in them or do something to move out of the feelings. It may take time but remember, in action there is hope.

Thoughts Create Emotions

Thoughts create emotions. No thought, equals no emotion. Control your thoughts and you control your emotions!

Conscious thought can diminish or increase the power of feelings. In the section on THE THOUGHT PROCESS, there is a well-known quotation which states that if you **"change your thoughts, you change your destiny"**. If you have allowed your emotions to take on a life of their own, then you are thinking the wrong thoughts. Change to the right thoughts. Don't let negative emotions live any longer than necessary in your mind.

Handling Emotions

The best way to make negative emotions go away is to embrace them - by looking at them and replacing them with happier feelings.

By doing so you also learn where in your body emotions live: your tummy, your heart, where? When you focus on an emotion, know what it feels like. When you know where it is and what it feels like and you focus on it, it will diminish. Try it, it does work as emotions cannot handle scrutiny. Of course you may find yourself having to do this over and over again but each time the fear returns it will remain for a shorter period and the gaps between appearances are extended.

INTROSPECTION

A slightly different introspection. The entire introspection will be about twelve minutes from when you have reached the alpha state. For two minutes bring anger to the fore – feel it. Then for two minutes reduce the anger and make yourself feel a sense of contentment. Then bring panic to your mind and for two minutes feel this. For the next two minutes, reduce the panic and bring back the feeling of happiness. Lastly do the same with guilt and ensure that you end the session feeling happy.

Write down what you discover: ……………………………………………………..
…………………………………………………………………………………………..

....
....

Remember, <u>emotions = energy in motion</u>, so bring emotions into the present and they are likely to diminish.

More on fear

When I refer to fear, I'm not talking about the fear of parachuting or bungee jumping, or the type of fear we have when sustaining physical injury. The fear that I refer to is that which holds us back from achieving the best that we can be. This fear lurks in our mind and is so subtle that most of the time we aren't aware of it and it appears in the form of our thinking or uttering, "No that is silly, I would not want to do that." Fear is an actor and does not announce that we are in fear. It emerges in the form of apathy.

The following is a list of fears that may ring true for you:

- Fear of failure
- Fear of success, which is really a fear of failure
- Fear of ridicule, because of possible failure
- Fear of rejection. This one is a self-esteem issue.
- Fear of being embarrassed. Once again, this is a self-esteem problem.
- Fear of relationships, or rather a fear that a relationship may end in disaster or a fear of being rejected by someone with whom you would like to be in a relationship with.
- Sometimes we become fearful if we are about to enter into an important meeting.
- Public speaking

Write down your fears: ....
....
....
....

STOP
Write down a time when you accepted a situation.
Do the same for a situation that you did not accept.
Reflect on them and feel the difference in your calmness.

....
....
....
....

What causes fear?

Self-doubt and a lack of self-worth are the biggest causes. Your above list can be overcome with better self-esteem.

When we are caught in the fear mind set, it is not the actual doing that scares us, <u>it is what could go wrong</u>. For example, if we fail at something it could be ridicule or embarrassment that is the concern. It is not the speaking in public that scares us, it is the making of mistakes while speaking in public.

You can't stop fear, but don't let it stop you!

Like emotions, fear can't be conquered by suggesting that it is not there, but it can be replaced with a determination that what you want to achieve is stronger than the fear. Will and desire can take you over, around, under or through fear.

Remember we discussed above the topic of **will**. To overcome fear, you must express your will, you must bolster your determination.

At this stage, I would like you to go back and re-read the entry story called *The Journey of Self* (at the front of the book). As you read it consider the fear elements and then return back to this point.

Journal notes: ....
....
....
....

STOP

Let's do a fear meditation. Compose yourself in the normal way and when ready cast your mind, like a net over the sea of your past. Summon a time when your mind would not allow you to undertake something. Bring it to your mind in the form of a doorway that you can't go through and so you back off. Then bring yourself to the doorway and for a second time back off. Now this time, before you reach the doorway, call your will, take a deep breath and let your determination rise, like steam from a kettle.
Launch yourself through the doorway – ah, you have done it.
Anytime you are aware of being held back, do this meditation.
The trick is in the calling forth of your will and determination, which is stronger than the fear.

Comments: ....
....
....
....
....
....
....
....
....

Love of self

It certainly is true that love for external things and people will ensure that you have a much more fulfilling life. But the love of the self is even more important. Without it, there can be no love beyond yourself. It all starts with how you see yourself!

LIFE'S LESSONS (again)

I speak a lot about life's lessons in this book. Acceptance of situations and issues are a part of life's lessons.

Journal: ....
....
....
....
....

Lessons = things to understand about yourself

Look at the following lessons:
- Until you forgive, you will not move on.
- Until you learn each life-lesson, they will recur with monotonous regularity in one form or another.
- In action there is hope.
- The Universal Source is benevolent.
- Life is long and everything improves for the better only if we allow it!
- By believing, you are not necessarily trusting.
- Running away from negative issues does not distance you from them.
- Knowing ThySelf is the start of taking responsibility.
- Negativity will curtail your life.

- Forgiving someone or an incident does not necessarily remove a script (above) that you are playing.

STOP
Can you add any more to the list?

....
....
....
....

Snapshot – 'In the orphanage'

After Mum saw the terror I felt at returning to the farm, she decided to marry Dad. She took control and got us kids away from the farm and those people as soon as possible. She placed us in an orphanage while she and dad made arrangements for the marriage and to buy a house. We were in the orphanage for six to eight months. I have several bad memories from this time. They are described elsewhere.

Life's lessons are experiences that arise for us to work through. They comprise of a thousand and one possibilities. No sooner do we overcome one experience than another appears. When we analyse our experiences either retrospectively or while they are happening, we learn about our shortcomings and our strengths, our attitudes, beliefs and vulnerabilities.

You may find that previously hidden abilities and gifts will emerge. These, if understood and processed, will enhance your power and your potential for success. Perhaps you will also discover impurities, addictions and fears. These could rise to the surface for the purpose of being seen, accepted and released or put to use. Your initial reaction may be to close up shop and escape as quickly as possible, to avoid the challenges, threats or embarrassments. Have faith in yourself and your intuition. Welcome the challenge. Freeing yourself from unwholesome habits and mindsets will help you build a good foundation of self-esteem and pave the way to joy and contentment.

STOP
Record at least one lesson that you have learned recently.

Journal: ....
....

....
....
....

Snapshot – Age 18 to 43 - Boozing

Is it any wonder I boozed? With all that happened to me, how could I avoid it? Sure I was able to hold down a job, but there were times when I was out of it for three or four days at a time. I even drank metholated spirits on one drunken occasion! Yuk! I shudder at the thought. And another night was spent in jail for, as the policeman said, "You are the drunkest bricklayer I have ever seen." This, of course was quite a boast as brickies are notorious for their drinking! Naturally, drinking did not help me, but it did numb my anger, mask the insecurities and bolster my self-esteem. On booze I was a legend in my own mind, a John Wayne and an Einstein all rolled into one.

Clearly, my purpose is to teach and help people but how could I accomplish this if I had not learnt the lessons the hard way? How could I use empathy if I had not felt

pain and remorse? I couldn't could I? Experience alone is not the teacher. It is the cognitive awareness of the experience and the action invoked that is the teacher. It is the living it and not the accumulation of information that teaches.

In Days of Old - A Fairytale

The following story is a metaphor of our struggle to find ourselves; it uses lots of symbolism. It is not the complete story but sufficient for the analogy. It is typical of the hidden messages that fairytales relay. If analysed, they can be about finding ourselves.

In days of old, when knights were bold, there lived a knight in not-too-shiny armour. He went by the name of Alphonce.

Alphonce, a poor knight, could not afford servants to clean his armour. He was so poor that he used to sleep in the woods. It rained a lot, which beat down with a drumming sound on his metal suit.

One bright summer day, with birds singing, Alphonce emerged from the forest to forage for scraps in the palace garbage bins. Not watching where he was going, he bumped into a damsel.

'Wach whare y goen, y big oaf,' she screeched. Alphonce was thunderstruck -- it was love at first sight. Other than a pea-sized carbuncle, massive beaked nose, hair like a sucked mango pip and pointy little chin, he thought her lovely. Her name was Fracila and she was a chambermaid of the Royal Guard. This was considered a lowly position, but there were perks!

A courtship followed that was to lead to marriage. It did not matter to her that he was a bit rusty; she had managed to secure her very own knight. He did not mind her castigating him for all kinds of reasons. However, Fracila suggested that he go off on an adventure, not only to prove himself, but mostly in search of a fortune on which to live. 'But I won't be able fight in rusty armour,' Alphonce squeaked.

Considering the problem, she said, 'I done a vaver fo the blacksmif, I'll git im to elp. Eel getcha clean. What sort of favour? Alphonce wondered.

She left and by and by arrived back with a sooty-skinned man, dragging a bag of tools. Introducing them, she said, 'Blacky, this is me hubby-to-be Alphonce; Alphonce, Blacky.'

Blacky got to work, polishing, scraping, scrubbing and painting and after a day and a half, our knight in shinier-but-still-battered armour, and with a borrowed donkey, was ready to set off for those distant shores to seek his fortune. Avoiding the carbuncle, he kissed Fracila and rode off into the wild, blue yonder.

Here we pause in our metaphor of life and its lessons.

- We started the story with Alphonce emerging from the forest rather worse for wear. Clearly his life did not work.
- An event, a catalyst, forced him to improve himself. Being an intrepid Knight, he took on the challenge.
- The cleaning of his armour is a metaphor for the cleaning up of his act.
- When he rode off, he began his journey of self-discovery.
- The fortune was the reward for the finding of self.

Now we will not go into all his trials and tribulations (lessons in life) in his search. Suffice it to say, there were many and we pick up the story some eight years later, when …

Alphonce returned, resplendent in brand new armour that would make any Knight of the Round Table proud. He rode regally upon a mount of such breeding and grace that he would become the talk of the land. Following Alphonce was an entourage of some fifty people. Clearly Alphonce had found his fortune.

Many of us have the image that tomorrow we will find ourselves. That some time in the future we will be happy and all will be well. In the story, this is what Alphonce accomplishes as he returns a hero. But, unless we do something today to improve our tomorrow, tomorrow will be just like today. Remember, this is a fairy tale and unless we solve our issues our armour will remain dull and rusty.

To continue …

Fracila was beside herself with joy and the anticipation of wealth. She batted her eyelashes at Alphonce as he dismounted. He seemed taller and stood with an eminence, full of confidence. Avoiding the carbuncle, he kissed her on the face and said, 'Fracila, we must talk ...'

In finding himself, Alphonce realised that he had grown beyond Fracila. While he had grown, she had remained the same. He learnt that he did not need her to make him happy and that he was in charge of his own destiny. Besides, there always has to be a twist in the tale, doesn't there?

Let see how it all ends up ...

And so it came to pass that the king issued a decree awarding Alphonce a parcel of land. He also gave him a stipend for his services to the Crown.

Alphonce gave Fracila a small pension. Nevertheless, she chose to retain her position as a chambermaid where, many a time, late at night, a knock on her door could be heard at her quarters and the clunking of metal as a sword was removed from some lonely Knight. And so they lived happily ever after...

Why we need to grow and move along:

I believe that our purpose is to move towards The Source. We are given lessons and have to overcome shortfalls, such as negativity, fear, anger and the rest. These negative traits (living towards the ego line) keep us from Source; they also keep us from enjoying our life.
God wants us to grow and learn. Without the lessons, we would become complacent. The main lesson I needed to overcome, was one of *'not being good enough'*. Therefore experiences were given to force me to look within in order to clear it. Yet, so many lessons were unnecessary. Had I learnt earlier that *'I am good enough',* these repetitive lessons would have ceased. Had I seen the real me and viewed beauty that resided within me, I wouldn't have required so many lessons. But more were to follow, because when I looked inside, all I saw were compost and worms. More gentle promptings came from The Universe, like repeating a year at school and being dyslexic. The lessons continued until I was able to overcome the limitations that I had placed upon myself.

You may pause here and ask, "What has this got to do with moving towards God?" The answer is quite simple. Until I could see the love and goodness in me, how could I see it elsewhere? How could I embrace a loving God if I saw only hate and limitation?

Our growth towards God is like a leaf in a busy brook, heading ever onwards to an unknown destination; sometimes getting snagged on rocks and at other times, being becalmed in backwaters or confronted with a waterfall. Like the leaf, we move towards the unknown, but unlike the leaf, we have the power to unsnag ourselves or move out of a backwater, to ride the rapids and move ever closer to perfection.

Life is like the journey of that brook – ultimately it ends in being absorbed by the source. This could happen over many lives.

INTROSPECTION

When you are composed, visualise your life (using the example of the leaf in the brook) and look where you have been snagged or where your life flowed briskly. Write down the major episodes that you find.

Journal: ....
....
....
....
....

> **STOP**
> **Look and see where in your life an event was a blessing**
> **even though at the time it did not seem so.**
> **Record it in your journal.**

Journal: ....
....
....
....
....

Remember, God does not take away from you, he merely opens a road to another direction.

SELF-ESTEEM = WORTH

Self-worth is the basis for spiritual advancement. When you accept your own natural capacity to be loved or to love, you also unknowingly accept the same qualities in The Supreme Being. Self-worth is a stepping-stone to self-love.

Other descriptions for a lack of self-esteem are inferiority complex or profound self-doubt.

If your mind is full of insecurity and inadequacy it is due to the fact that these thoughts have dominated your thinking over a long period of time. These must be replaced with positive patterns.

Snapshot – Ages 7 to 16 - 'Not Good Enough'

A lot of the time as I was growing up, I had a funny feeling in my stomach and thought it felt like squirming snakes. The feeling was so prevalent, that a lot of the time I was not even aware of them. Another name for the snakes could be called anxiety.

I remember when I was about eleven I was playing down the road at a friend's house. His name was Gary Prentice. On this Sunday afternoon we were extracting tadpoles from a pond in his backyard. His mother came down to us and said to Gary, "We are going for a drive to Palm Beach, so come in and clean up". She said to me, "You must go home".

Upon hearing this, Gary complained and said that he wanted me to come and so his mother relented and off we went.

The Prentices were an odd assortment of characters. There was Uncle George who was a blind kindly soul, but as blank to understand as his sightless stare. There was Granny, who no doubt could have doubled as the Wicked Witch in Snow White.

Gary's mother was a measly-looking thing who was prone to frowning or not showing interest in anything. And Gary's dad, Mr Prentice, was a wisp of a man who was more bent than upright. When he spoke it was with a squeaky sort of voice. There was also a sister or two but I don't remember much about them.

In fact, I did not even like Gary much, but he was fortunate enough to have a tadpole farm, which later became a frog farm.

Their house, which I kept out of, always had a smell about it. To this day I can remember it but can't put a name to it, but it was a smell that I hated.

And so I found myself squashed in the middle of this creepy bunch, heading up the coast.

An hour later, once there, Mother Prentice said, "Who wants ice cream?" There were "yes's" all around. So the three adults scratched in their pockets and brought out an assortment of coins. We all gave our orders. The Witch and Mother Prentice went into the shop and soon emerged with a bunch of ice creams. One was handed out to each person, but when it came to mine, there was the Witch with only one ice cream and as she licked it she said, "Sorry, there was not enough money". And so, they all sat and licked and ooh-aaad while I was lucky enough to be able to watch.

On the outside I said nothing, but my insides felt like I had been punched. Now remember, just before this story I was telling you about the squirming in the gut. Well that's when I first became aware of it. It was a feeling that I got to know well and it lived with me for many years. Because I was putting out to the universe that I wasn't worthy, that's exactly what I got. I was continually short-changed.

> **STOP**
> **Do you relate to, or have you also experienced, a type of squirming in your belly?**
> **Perhaps you can identify with another feeling.**
> **If so, how often do you feel it?**

....
....
....
....
....
....

Poor health is often a result of low self-esteem. You work it out - do you think you can be in good health if you always feel down as a result of low self-worth?

Your perpetual fear thoughts, even those below your subconscious, raise your adrenalin. Adrenalin releases glycogen from the liver. Adrenalin that remains in the system for prolonged periods is destructive. It is much like taking aspirin; the system can handle small doses, but taken in large quantities, it has a toxic effect.

CONFIDENCE = Moving in the right direction

We are born without the fears that rule us later on and so we are willing to try almost anything. But as life progresses, we develop fears. As fear reduces our confidence, we need to recapture the fearlessness that we had as children.

Confidence comes from a thorough knowledge of who we are. Confidence comes from practice and experience.

Previously, we discussed how our life consists of many different boxes. In some areas we are confident, in others, timid.

In a business meeting you may exude great ability and confidence. You get out of the meeting and bump into Mary, whom you have been attracted to for months. You blush and get all flustered. Knowing our boxes (as given above) is really important. When each separate one is improved, our level of confidence grows accordingly.

There are times when we are confident and at other times we are not. Look at the times when your confidence was low. If you find a pattern, work on those areas (boxes) that need attention. Remember what we said about being in the present moment and also what we said about emotions merely being thoughts. When feeling a lack of confidence, put yourself into the present moment and you will see it is easier to replace negative thoughts with positive ones.

> **STOP**
> **Make a list - on the left write down areas where you know you are confident and on the right, areas where you feel compromised.**
> **Look for patterns in both.**
> **In the areas where you feel insecure,**
> **what can you do to turn them around?**
> **What can you do to make yourself more confident?**

....
....
....
....
....

INTROSPECTION

When in a relaxed state, bring to your mind one of the insecure areas that you have just taken note of. Then tell your mind to change the feeling of negativity to that of being confident. See yourself participating in this area in a confident manner. Take as long as you need, but ensure that you only finish the introspection when you feel confident. You will need to do this introspection for each of the areas where you lack confidence and you will also need to do several of introspections per topic.

Journal: ....
....
....
....
....

Confidence and Being Positive

It is impossible to be negative and have deep confidence in yourself. Confidence will increase as you clear the negative rubbish from your mind.

If you have no confidence in yourself, you are twice defeated in the race of life. With confidence you have won even before you have started.
— Marcus Garvey

STOP
Can you see that being positive, where you take back your power, can help with your confidence?

Journal: ....
....
....
....
....

Confidence and 'so-called' Mistakes

Confidence can be likened to an iceberg. If something goes wrong it melts a bit and when lots of things go wrong it melts even more. When things are good the berg re-forms. By knowing ourselves, as this book suggests, we will understand our weaknesses. By knowing our weaknesses we can look for methods or patterns of behaviour to overcome them. There will be fewer things going wrong. Therefore the iceberg (confidence) is less likely to melt. But having said this, with awareness, every experience can help you to win.

Strong confidence in yourself comes from many things going right. A lack of success results in lowered confidence.
True confidence then is an unshakable belief in yourself. This leads to *boldness*. Confidence has to be claimed!

STOP
Look at your life and try to see when your confidence regressed or grew according to events and circumstances.

Journal: ....
....
....
....
....

Confidence is not something we are born with; it is learned and developed.

SELF-CONCEPT = Limitations or Power,
                depending on how you see yourself

How we view ourselves ensures that we behave in a manner consistent with that view.

STOP
Introspect and try and see yourself as others see you.
Do this in different scenarios, such at work, socially
or when playing sport.
Remember that we do not know how life really is.
We only know how we represent it to ourselves.

....
....
....
....

We don't have only one self-concept. We have many, which make up the complete whole. These beliefs are derived from how we see ourselves within each of our boxes.

"Friendship with oneself is all important, because without it one cannot be friends with anyone else" - Eleanor Roosevelt. She also said, "No one can hurt you without your consent."

Self reliance

Another benefit of Knowing ThySelf is that we achieve self-reliance. Self-reliance is about taking responsibility and control of our thoughts and therefore control of our lives. When we are reliant on ourselves we no longer have fantasies about being rescued, either by a partner or perhaps by winning the lotto!

Snapshot – Age 6 until the present

BEING DYSLEXIC (This is an article that I wrote for a magazine)

Damn it. Once again I bank 103 instead of 301 bucks. I'm dyslexic and, as you read this, you'll see that being dyslexic has governed my entire life, sometimes in amusing ways, like the time when I thought I would try my hand at Internet dating. Instead of selecting the contender's age range of 36 to 47. I flagged 36 to 74. Can you imagine my horror when a toothless, prune-faced geriatric beamed at me as I opened my e-mail?

Dyslexia is derived from two Greek words, Dys – meaning poor or inadequate and Lexis – words or language. According to research the cortex has six basic layers, with layer one having essentially no cells, but dyslexics typically have bunches of cells in layer one.

It seems that dyslexia is a disease of the fortunate as research indicates that you have to be above average intelligence to have it. And here is the killer for you feminists -- males are three times more likely to have it than females. But then I am not too sure about the research ... such as, why would they use mice to look at encoding phonological or temporal processing?

A friend once asked me how my dyslexic brain functions. 'It works,' I told her, 'as if it were correct and the rest of the world wrong. It has a method of its own, like that of some sort of strange animal species that evolved in an unknown pocket of wilderness. I have no problem with maths and can add as quickly as anyone. But when I am trying to spell a word it is as though the connections come adrift. I get stuck in a sort of limbo. This is probably the reason why I spell the same word in a document many different ways, and each looks correct to me. My mind won't be boxed in and limit the word to only one spelling.'

In my first year of school I could not form letters of the alphabet, like prissy Mary could. I moved my tongue out of my mouth with the effort, but the result was still a mess. It was as if the pencil had a will of its own. This was the start of my being labelled 'different'. I was held back at the end of that first year, to 'try again' with another bunch of kids.

In time I discovered that there were more and more things that I couldn't cope with. The label 'different' was later amended to 'dunce'. Yet I didn't feel stupid. But as time went on I told myself, 'Maybe this is what being stupid is like.'

The school system, and the ability to form neat r's or j's, was the measure. School is still the standard by which our intellectual capacity, or lack of, is gauged. It didn't take long before I lost faith in school, thought of myself as hopeless and blocked learning even more. I developed a brittle self-esteem and became an unfulfilled and angry person.

If there was one area in my life that helped to salvage some self-respect it was on the sports field, as I fared better than most. Without the balance of sport, I would have been in a sorry state.

A new school year was always interesting as the incoming teacher either unconsciously or consciously classified the children. It was never long before I was relegated to the back of the class, considered a waste of time. Provided I behaved I was generally ignored. That was forty odd years ago. Schools may be different today.

Of course, I wasn't quiet and well-behaved and through expressing myself I disrupted the class. So not only did the teacher consider me 'slow', but a nuisance as well.

Year after sorry year passed with me sliding further back into academic oblivion. I became angrier and more rebellious. Year three of high school saw 'them' putting pressure on me to leave. This was just fine by me and, as ironic as it may seem, I left school to get an education.

Only later, when Mum saw the same elements in my young brother, did she set out to find an answer. Her studies culminated in her becoming a remedial teacher. By that time I had left home. Visiting one night, she explained about dyslexia. I'd never heard of the word and thought, 'so what?' She wanted to train me with remedial techniques but, being touchy about the matter, I made all sorts of excuses. I was fine as a bricklayer and occasional drunk.

Fortunately, as the years passed, I gained confidence in myself as a person. The inadequacies receded and became less important. My child-like writing, atrocious spelling and the mixing of numbers did not concern me any more.

The brain is a wonderful organism and over the years mine has, to a degree, trained itself to reverse errors. For instance, I might be looking for 93 and upon seeing the number say 'ah, there's 39', but I know it is 93 as an instantaneous reversal would have taken place.

At one stage in my work I conducted presentations to executives with lots of notes on flip charts. Seldom was there a time when a dyslexic slip-up didn't make an appearance. An example could be when I started to write the word bank, but it appeared on the board as bnak. There were other times when bank appeared as nbka. In other words, I would write first the b and then the n, which I'd squeeze in to the left of the b, and so on.

When I produce any of these unintended gems I'm not aware of the awkward sequence. In my mind it is normal spelling. The adjustments are made without conscious thought. In fact, I may only realise something abnormal has happened if I notice the audience casting flabbergasted looks towards the board as if to say, 'Whoa, did you see that?'

I'm often amused at the Universe's sense of humour when it conjured me as a dyslexic person while laying a path to writing. Or is it rather the intelligence of the Universe? And what about timing? I couldn't have managed in commerce if I'd been born twenty years earlier. My hand-written correspondence wouldn't have been of an acceptable standard. The corporates would have disposed of me, like a pack of wild dogs abandoning an injured or aged member. I was given the handicap and, at the same time, a personal computer with a phenomenal spell-check!

On the subject of machines, an ATM can provide a fascinating experience for me. I usually have no problem getting my pin number out of my head. But if, at the time, someone near me mentions another number, for instance a telephone number, then my mind becomes jumbled and I can't get the pin number into the ATM correctly. I remember watching helplessly as one card was consumed, never to be seen again by an overzealous machine as a result of my confusing the number. When I get the jumbles, it's best for me to leave the ATM, reformat the hard disk of my brain and return later.

Continuing with the answer to my friend, I told her that my mind has difficulty deciphering gothic or fancy script. Most cursive writing is gobbledygook and has to be read to me. But I also told her that being dyslexic has forced me to become the achiever that I am today. If I am in front of a group of executives, I don't care about my scrawl. I have learned to establish my own worth, and not to allow society to provide the rules by which my value is measured. Empowered, I rose from being an almost illiterate bricklayer at twenty-two, to owning and managing my own computer software company, where I designed software for business use.

It is late, 25:12 a.m., and time for bed.

STOP
If you wanted to start your own business,
would you do it on your own or with a partner?

Your answer..
....
....
....
....

Your answer to the above question will give you an idea of your trust in yourself.

STOP
Now that you have answered the above three questions, work through
your life and identify times when you have been self-reliant.
Look for trends. Record all these thoughts in your journal.

Journal: ....
....
....
....
....

If you want to achieve true freedom, then it is imperative that you assume as much self-reliance as possible. **Anything that you are dependent upon is a limitation.**

INTROSPECTION

In this introspection, look at the main areas of your life to see if you have any dependencies. Record them in your journal.

You cannot be self-reliant with any issue if your actions do not match your desires. What lets you down are your negative thoughts.

Journal: ....
....
....
....
....

Not I, nor any one else, can travel that road for you. You must travel it for yourself.
- Walt Whitman, 1819 – 1892
(American philosopher, poet and writer)

Envy = Our small selves

STOP
Have you ever contemplated someone else's good fortune in a manner that reduces your self worth?

....
....
....
....

Snapshot - Ages 3 to 4 - *No 'Sveeties' for you*

While being incarcerated on The German's farm, one of his kids had a birthday party and so some of the children from the area came for the day. I had never been to a party, nor seen so many cakes and sweets all in one place. Of course I got excited and buzzed with glee.

My mind is still furnished with the scene – the table with all the wonders was under a lean-to. On one side there was a laundry or washroom and the other was the back end of the house. A door with a fly-screen led into the kitchen. The kids were dotted around the table and were climbing in with excitement that only a children's party can muster.

I was at an age where I could just see above the table, so most of the enticing items were at eye height. There were jellybeans (still my favourite, especially the black ones) cakes of rainbow colours; liquorice lay in lengths across the table, like juicy black snakes. There was a range of soft drinks, all with their own unique colour. Of course at that time I did not know their names or tastes, but I knew them to be good.

To start with I was timid, as I didn't know what to expect, but taking my lead from the other kids, I reached out for a sweet. The German must have been watching from the kitchen for as I latched onto one he burst out of the screen door and said while pointing at me, "Nein, nein, no, not you, no sveety for you." He then moved me away from the table, but not so far that I could not see all the kids enjoying themselves. I was told, "Stand and vatch." He then said to the other children, "It's OK, eat."

As a writer I do not know if I have the ability to describe how I felt watching the other kids enjoying themselves. I cannot blame them as they only did what was natural, but the hurt and confusion was greater than what my grasp of English can describe.

Envy announces that you have self-esteem issues

Envy and resentment is begrudging someone else's luck, ability or possessions. It creates discontentment.

Envy is not you. Feeling envious is not living in the present moment. If you were in the present moment, you could never feel belittled as a result of someone else having something you don't. Nor would you fall prey to the negativity resulting from your belief that you are not capable of doing something that someone else can. When you are envious your focus is external, not internal. Envy is associated with limited self-esteem. If you frequently suffer from envy, re-read the sections on self-esteem and self-reliance.

Being envious will take your eye off the ball.

Envy is not taking responsibility or control of your thoughts. When envy ends in resentment you give your power away. You create blockages.

If you find yourself consistently contemplating someone else's good fortune in a manner that reduces your self-worth, you must do your best to address this and change this part of yourself.

Journal: ....
....
....
....
....

Envy is merely a symptom of negativity!

Love looks through a telescope; envy looks through a microscope.
– Josh Billings

STOP
Record any feelings of envy that you have had.
Try to understand why you were envious.

Journal: ....
....
....
....
....

THE POWER OF CHOICE = The correct direction

Choice, the power of; is one of my favourite subjects, one that is much neglected. Understanding the power of choice can really empower you. After all, where you are in life has nothing to do with your destiny. It is the result of past choices or not choosing.

There is a correlation between responsibility and the ability to choose. Similarly, realising that you do have alternatives from which to choose enhances your self-reliance.

> **STOP**
> Think about your day today. You may have had a choice
> to be nice to someone who annoyed you or got in your way.
> **What was that choice?**
> **And what were the implications of that choice?**

....
....
....
....

Responsibility – the ability to respond

For this discussion, we do not refer to making choices in the sense of which job you may take or whom to marry, although you do need to be self-reliant to make these type of choices correctly and with confidence. Choice as reflected here is used as a tool to manage yourself, a method to empower your life. Choice in this context is the choice of what to think or not to think. You are given free will to choose how you perceive something - the choice to choose life and happiness, negative thoughts, positive thoughts, wealth or poverty thoughts.

Attitude

Attitude is something that you have absolute control over. The choice of your attitude is up to you.

> **STOP**
> **Was it your script that steered you towards the wrong choices?**

Journal: ....
....
....
....

- Right choice, right outcome; wrong choice, choose again.
- You are where all your choices have led you.
- Making choices is a talent that must be developed.

- The more choices you make the better you will get at it.

> **STOP**
> **Get some paper and write in big bold letters,**
> ***This morning I am positive and happy.***
> **Place this on the floor, between your bed and the toilet,**
> **so when you head that way after waking up you will pick it up**
> **and apply the right 'mood'. When you put on your clothes,**
> **also dress in the right mood. Then wear it around with you.**
> **See what a difference it will make to your day.**

"The Lord helps those who help themselves." You choose whether you want to help yourself or not. When we think that we have no choice, we become victims. In other words, if your mind thinks there is no reasonable alternative, then your mind will consider you a victim and treat you as such. As you create your own reality, it is crucial that you choose positive self-empowering thoughts. Sometimes you will get lost and not see it but there is always a choice!

What do you think of the above paragraph?

....
....
....
....

Karma is choice, or choice becomes karma!

> **STOP**
> **How do you start each day?**

Each morning you have two choices - happy or sad, positive or negative, empowered or disempowered. The choice sets the tone for the day.

How do you start each day? ....

....
....
....
....

> **STOP**
> **How do you think the power choice can**
> **help you in your immediate life?**

....
....
....
....

> **STOP**
> How often have you made a decision based
> on fear or negativity? At the time you may not
> have been conscious that it was fear or negativity influencing
> your decision, but in retrospect, you could see that it was.

....
....
....
....

Choice and Emotion

If you make a choice or decision that is based on an emotion, then you need to understand and take responsibility for it. If the emotion derives from negativity, such as fear, anger or jealousy, then it is likely the end result will be negative.

Journal notes: ....
....
....
....
....
....
....
....

At the start of this section on CHOICE, the power of, I said that this is one of my favourite sections of the book.

> **STOP**
> Why do you think that this section on choice is so important to me?

Journal: ....
....
....
....
....

Without the power of **choice** I would have remained a bricklayer. Without the power of **choice,** I could have become an alcoholic. Because of the power of **choice**, I left behind relationships that were not serving me well. With the knowledge that life offers **choices**, I became a writer and teacher. Because I had a **choice** I was able to empower myself and reconstruct my life.

Journal notes: ....
....
....
....
....

The power of choice and being conscious

The best decisions created by the power of choice are those made with consciousness - being in the present moment consciousness.

Letting go

It is fitting that **letting go** follows on from 'The Power of Choice' as there will be times when you will have to make a conscious choice to let go. It may be the letting go of a person, a life style, a position or a belief.

STOP
Think about this and take note of what you decide.

....
....
....
....

Raging River

If you were clinging to an over-turned boat and being dragged down a raging river; and if you knew that there was a waterfall up ahead, what would you do? You are likely to **let go**. You may cling to the boat for as long as possible as it may seem to be the best security you have.

Now, what if you were arguing with your adolescent son about something. You feel that your viewpoint is correct but by pushing the principle you could lose him. Would you continue the lecture?

You probably came to the conclusion that you would **let go**, but that was in a state of rationality. Now, throw in some emotion and ego and guess what? Most would push the lesson aside and not see the point.

It is a rare person who is able to see clearly at the expense of a principle and ego. Until we let go, we can't move on, nor will we grow. Letting go is about forgiveness (refer to the section on Forgiveness).

STOP
When you can let go it means that you have understood a lesson.
Look for times in your life when you didn't let go of something:
an argument, a relationship that was dysfunctional.
Try to re create the feeling that you had within and dissipate it.

Journal: ....
....
....
....

Snapshot – Aged 8 - *Hives*

Not beehives but the type that grow on your legs and arms, that cover your body, dozens of them, all itching and festering into sores once the top is scratched off. These are what I had from about ages five to twelve.

Hives, I have since read, are the result of stress or a nervous disposition. At the time, Mum used to dab them with calamine lotion, a pink blob that did not seem to have any effect, other than making it look like I had 'gay measles'.

Metaphysical counsellor and author, Louise Hay, says that '**hives are small hidden fears.**'

Perhaps the hardest time to let go is when we are in a **comfort zone** as a result of fear. We are afraid to let go, to move on, be on our own, start that business, re-locate.

If you have ever been strong enough to do the moving on, it is likely that your *personal growth* would have benefited by the move. Before you moved on, there would have been an inner voice saying to you, *'This situation is not right, get out'*. It is likely that there would have been another one saying, *'No, stay put, what if it does not work? What if the money doesn't come in? What if I don't make friends?'* And a thousand other what- if's. The initial 'gut feeling' voice was your intuition then your logical mind kicked in. The mind that blocks, the one that is ruled by negativity, the one that limits you in your achievements. It is the same mind that says, 'I can't speak in public', or 'It is too hard for me to do this or that'.

STOP
Are you brave enough to move on when
that little voice tells you it is time?

Journal: ....
....
....
....
....

Listening and taking notice of that little voice is taking responsibility for yourself and ultimately a better life. It requires faith in yourself to manage and create. By the way, that little voice is your Higher Self watching out for you.

INTROSPECTION

Can you trust your ability to manage and create? Go into a contemplation and think of a time where you needed to trust your ability to manage and create. Record in your journal what you discover.
Be careful that the prompting from your inner voice really serves you and is not an excuse to always get on your bicycle and run away from every challenging situation. You obviously wouldn't break up a healthy lifelong marriage because of a few challenging months.

Journal: ....
....
....
....
....

Change

Heraclitus, a Byzantine emperor c. 575 – 641, said that, "There is nothing permanent except change".

For life to be full and stimulating there must be change. Whether the change is tough or good, it is likely to lead to growth and wisdom. Change by choice means dumping the security blanket, the dependency. It is rocking the boat and challenging complacency. You will be forced to expand your ideas.

Life's wonderful processes will force change upon you, drag you from the known into the unknown, the comfortable to the uncomfortable and back to the comfortable. It all has to do with life's lessons.

Most people are apprehensive about change. The thought of change is associated with negativity. Remember change usually works out for the best.

Like it or not, there will be change in your life. Look at the advancement in technology over the last twenty years. Look at the change that has been forced upon you. Don't panic: embrace it, especially changing yourself. If you don't change, you stagnate.

Imagine if you did not change over the next ten years. You would be thinking the same thoughts and nursing the same ideas – the current grudges would still be ruling your life, as would your fears. There would be no new subjects for you to ponder on. You will probably have the same friends, talk about the same topics (same rubbish, different day). How sad, limiting and boring!

As William Joyce (writer) said: "A great many people think they are thinking when they are merely rearranging their prejudices".

It is essential to change in order to advance. Never allow yourself to fall into a complacent comfort zone. Growth and expansion of thoughts is an ongoing process – there is no point of arrival. Just when you think you've arrived, there is a new starting point.

You do not have to seek change. Self-exploration is the best catalyst for change. Once you understand who you are and who you want to be, it will come naturally, provided you are listen to your intuitive inner voice. Exciting isn't it?

By growing and allowing these transformations, the negative effects of your past will begin to have less dominance in your life and you will grow beyond the negative hold the past has on you.

STOP
Think about when you were afraid of a change but it worked out for the best.

....
....
....

"When you're through changing, you're through."

— Bruce Barton

STOP
Look at a time in your life when you regretted not making a change? How does it make you feel now?

Journal: ....
....
....
....
....

In the event of a change in circumstances, look at the benefits of the decision, not at what you may be losing or leaving. See the gain!

Journal: ....
....
....
....

....
....
....
....

Unplanned change always leads to learning.

South Africa - A Changed Country

An example of a wonderful change is in South Africa. Before the abolition of Apartheid in 1994, when the African National Congress took control of government, most of the white population were apprehensive and did not want to go down that road of uncertainty.

Previously, the white ruling party was able to hold on to power, not because what they were doing was correct, but because the white people of the country were scared of change. They were fearful that the country would become communistic, be run by a bunch of despots and that they would be driven into the Indian Ocean. Through pressure from the international community, change was inevitable and with it the economy improved. The confidence levels of the community (as shown by the confidence index) grew. If a poll was run where whites were given a chance to go back to pre-1994 rule, I believe that 95% would not choose to go back to those 'dark' Apartheid days. Yet when they were in what is now referred to as those 'dark days', people clung on to the 'dark' for fear of change.

Evolution

Evolution is the natural order. We humans, within our lifetime, are also evolving. We are the creators of our very own individual evolution. We evolve through moving from the right of the ego line towards the left. It is the ever-constant growth towards Source and a better life.

Evolution has taken man from an ape to what he is now. Evolution can take you from a life that does not work to one that does.

FATE = Cop out

I believe that handing your life over to fate is a cop out. Assigning your future to fate is shirking your responsibility. It is 'allowing' something to happen at a time when perhaps, with a proactive approach and right action, the final result could be different, beneficially different. By taking control, you are more likely to have a better outcome.

If you think an outcome is inevitable, then it will be!

Belief in fate is a severe limitation.

> **STOP**
> **Do you believe in fate?**
> **Have you allowed that belief to influence something that you could have changed?**

....
....
....
....

Believing in fate indicates that you think that all situations are pre-ordained and that you have no control over circumstances. With this belief, it follows that you must assume that there is 'someone upstairs' orchestrating your every move, like some giant chess match, plotting your downfall or success. It assumes that God has not given you *free will* (or choice) in which case we might as well be imbecilic robots and allow the Universe to move our pawns or castles on the chess board of life. It goes against the belief that man was made in the image of God, and because God creates, we are co-creators. If we were ruled by fate, we would not have the ability to create.

If our lives were controlled by fate, what would be the reason for living or the purpose of this grand experiment of the Universe? Where would the learning and growth come from and how would mankind develop? What would be in it for The Universal Intelligence? And lastly, who would decide that a person has a car accident while another wins the lottery?

> **STOP**
> **Ponder what you have just read and form your own opinions.**

Journal: ....
....
....
....

Fate is a myth, one that reduces your ability to effectively produce the outcomes in life that you seek. You are in control of your own destiny. Yes, there may be external influences and of course there are lessons, but the direction you travel is the direction you set for yourself. You are born into certain circumstances, but it is up to you and your thought processes that determine whether you remain stuck in your circumstances or move on.

The God-in-me is the master of my fate. If you believe in fate then your belief will become your fate.

If it was not meant to be, then it was not meant to be.

STOP
Have you heard this? Do you say it?

If so, how often? ....
....
....
....

This saying is debilitating and will disempower you.

The difference between man and beast is that man was blessed with consciousness and was given 'free will' and the intelligence to express it.

STOP
Will you let life direct you or are you going to create yourself as an exceptional person?

Journal notes: ....
....
....
....
....

SUCCESS

Snapshot – Age 4 - *The Beach*

There is no reason for an orphanage to be an unhappy place, yet ours was. It was grim and without any spontaneity. There was never any singing (kids love singing) or joy. This can only be ascribed to the people who cared for us, and the direction that came from management.

On the afternoon in question, all of us children were put onto a bus and taken to a local beach.

Once there, instead of being able to run around, we were herded into a line, where we walked up and down the sand. I remember seeing a family, where a mother and father sat with their children who were about my age. I had the clear feeling that they were 'normal' kids and that we were somehow 'abnormal'. This feeling came as a direct result of the orderlies that looked after us.

We wandered along the beach in a kind of grim silence. The only difference between us and prisoners was that we had no chains.

The day should have been wonderful. We could have had such fun, but we didn't. In fact, I came back feeling like some sort of shame had settled on me - a shame that the rest of the world could see.

Many years later, I read a newspaper article written by a journalist who had been abandoned to the same orphanage as we were. She was there at the same time but being older her memories of the place would have been more concise. In her story, she entwined the current workings of the establishment with her memories of growing up there. She was scathing in her descriptions, saying how there was no compassion or love offered by the staff.

Success is fulfilment and when you consider yours, don't listen to what society suggests as the standard. You must understand what is important to you.

STOP
Is your position or money an indication of success?

....
....
....

I consider success a state of mind. Does your success or state of mind make you happy? If you are not happy, how can you be fulfilled? Being famous or living in a big house has nothing to do with success. If you live a fear-based life, then *you* 'have not made it'. In forming your own definitions of success, ask the questions: Do you enjoy life? Will you continue to enjoy life?

Identifying with money or power is not nearly as precious as identifying with happiness, love and contentment. When you create your own understanding of success, be true to yourself, not what society expects. Flattery is an ego issue as are the labels that go around. Be careful of your illusions, cravings and ambitions. When you read this section on success, keep these thoughts in mind.

Recognise that you have the courage within you to fulfil the purpose of your birth. — *Gurumayi Chidvilasananda*

Can you say that you have led a fulfilling life if you have not achieved anything? No you can't, so roll up your sleeves and become triumphant at something. How many goals have you accomplished over the last few years? Keep setting and achieving them.

Success is not measured by one or two aspects. As can be seen from the above, it is many things.

From now on, be your very own "Very Important Person" and then you are more likely to be the success you strive for.

Success is hard, failure is easy

To achieve success, we have to work for it, whereas failure is usually brought on by a lack of effort, either mental or physical. Success takes risk and guts. Most people don't have the strength of character to take risks. Success takes character; failure is being less responsive.

If you want success, you will have to meet it head on, fight for it and beat it with a stick. You get failure by being meek.

Defining Success

This section on success suggests that you evaluate what success means to you. You identify what is important to you. This encompasses family life, how hard you want to work, your health and dozens of other topics. To be successful, you need to take time to evaluate. You need to know in your mind what is important and what is not. By doing so, you begin the process that will take you to that fulfilment. As there are likely to be many different topics, set goals and time frames for each. Know that these aspirations may take time, and do not attempt to make too many changes at once.

Lao Tzu says: "The longest journey starts with a single step."
Henry Norwill says: "In the right direction!"

Don't listen to what others say you can't do and you will never pay attention to their limitations again.
- Unknown

INTROSPECTION

So you want success? Have you defined what it is to you?
Introspect on what you want to achieve in terms of your success.

Record in your journal your initial thoughts, then when you have finished the book, go back and re-evaluate.

Journal notes: ……………………………………..…………………………………..
………………………………………………………………………………………………..
………………………………………………………………………………………………..
………………………………………………………………………………………………..
………………………………………………………………………………………………..

Success - keeping on trying

Trial and error is how we learn. Trying again and again opens up the opportunity for eventual success. I remember reading in the paper about a woman who was determined to meet her man. In one year she went out with one hundred and twenty men. She accepted every date and encouraged each glance; sure enough within a year she had met the man whom she married and had several children with him. She even wrote a book about her 'exploits'.

So like the dating woman, the greater the number of attempts you make, the more likely you are to achieve victory. The example of Thomas Edison (1847 – 1931) is a great case in point. Apparently he was unsuccessful in creating the light bulb in over two thousand experiments. Yet the more he tried, the closer he got until he eventually succeeded.

Let's say you were a sales person and assume that you had three potential sales orders. You would not do as well as the sales person who has six or ten. So when it comes to success, just keep trying, don't give up and the numbers will work in your favour.

In Japan, it is well known that the average businessman goes broke five times before he achieves success.

> **STOP**
> **How many times would you allow yourself to attempt to run a business or something of value to you, knowing that you may need five attempts?**

....
....
....
....
....
....

Success is Ongoing

Success in life is not a one-time win. It is the consistent and ongoing attainment of many small goals. They must be in line with the 'success criteria' that you wrote out above.

Success is Not only One Thing

Like the many boxes that make up your character, to be successful, in terms of the definition of success given at the start of this section, requires fulfilment in as many of your boxes as possible. You cannot say you are a successful person if you are the General Manager of your company but have miserable relationships or low self-esteem. Therefore, when you look for the meaning of success in your life, cover all aspects of yourself.

Success and Goals

You can only measure success by your own pre-determined criteria, not against what others have achieved. While it is great to have mentors and archetypes of people you admire, don't use their achievements as *your* milestones.

Success is a consequence of choice - choice of attitude, choice of self-reliance and choice of belief. It is the choice to set off in a direction while monitoring your progress.

It stands to reason that to be successful you must know what you want to achieve. Do you have clear goals? (Refer to goals below) Do you have a well-defined methodology to achieve your goals? Success comes from knowing what is required and acting upon it.

Success does not lie in the achievement of the goal but in the journey towards the goal. As each goal is reached, new goals need to be set.

Success and Challenge

Remember the best fruit is out on the limb. — *Unknown*

We can only achieve success if we accept the challenge and assume responsibility for what we want to achieve. We don't know what we are capable of unless we accept the challenge and test our capabilities. You may be pleasantly surprised at how much you can achieve when you are determined. The overcoming of obstacles is a function of your personal evolution, of whom or what you want to be.

STOP
What challenges have you avoided in your life?
And had you not avoided them, how different could your life have been?
Are you a mover and shaker? If not, why not?

....
....
....
....
....
....

Snapshot - *My Work Life*

This section is about success and challenge and so let me tell you about some work-related challenges of mine.

I started my computer software business some nineteen years ago, full of enthusiasm, with lots of ideas and I was going to get rich. I had a false bravado. I *was prepared to face the challenge of being under financed, but the real challenge was the hidden one – the one of self-worth. It was a challenge that at the time I had not overcome. I went broke, but as you will learn under the section **Failure**, there is no such thing as failure, that is, unless you give up. I started again, this time with even less money, plus the debt – this was an even greater challenge. But I made it.*

An ongoing challenge of my company, was the building of new software products, and then seeing if they will sell. Our modus operandi *was to sniff out opportunities for a programme. If it felt right, we threw large sums of money into building it. It would take two or three years from conception to a finished product and at any stage, there was no real way of knowing if the product would be a success. It was only after we presented it to the business community did we see if we had a rising star or a dog – this was the challenge.*

I recently read theses on IT companies, specifically software houses, and the research suggested that the worldwide failure rate for software companies was 87% - the challenge of being one of the 13% was one that I won.

You can't wait for inspiration. You have to go after it with a club.
— Jack London 1876 – 1916,
(author of 'Call Of The Wild' and 'White Fang')

It is not what happens to you in life that is important, it is how you react to it. Are you up to the challenge?

Journal notes: ....
....
....
....
....

It's kind of fun to do the impossible.
— Walt Disney 1901 – 1966
(filmmaker and creator of Disneyland)

We were born to succeed. We have been given all the tools to overcome any problems that confront us. There are no obstacles that we cannot conquer. It is the will of man that determines whether the obstacles are insurmountable or conquerable. It is determination that will drive us forward after defeat. The will is supported by the courage that is generated from within.

What would you like to do that you may think is impossible? ....
....
....
....
....

Success and Belief

You see it when you believe it.
— Dr Wayne Dyer (author, teacher)

In other words, you will only achieve something once you believe it, not 'I will believe it when I see it'. By the way, I highly recommend Dyer's books.

As a man thinketh, so he goes. — Proverbs 23:7

Ask, and it shall be given you; seek, and ye shall find; knock and it shall be opened unto you. — Matthew 7:7

Hold your head high and be the best you can, even when life seems to fall apart - face each difficulty with the confidence that tomorrow will be better. You will have a greater likelihood of achieving that ultimate success, if you never give up. Trust is the key.

Achievers don't envy. They know they have the ability to create or earn anything they want.

The Tools Versus Who You Are

The final deciding factor of whether or not you are successful in your life is who you are, *not what you have*. You may have a wonderful education, but education is merely a tool. You may have wealth. Wealth is also just a tool. We all have different abilities that we can utilise, but it is our thought processes that put them to effective use. Tools alone will not bring lasting success. Other aids such as contacts, an ability to work hard or being organised will all help but only with the right mindset and attitude will the desired manifestation occur.

And whatever things you ask in prayer, believing, you will receive.
                                                            - Matthew 21:22

The operative word here is 'believing'. When you do the work, it can happen. No one person has every strength and attribute. We all have limitations. Know them well, but do not let them stand in the way. Make the most of what you have and believe that you can do whatever you set out to do.

Remember, I am dyslexic, yet it has not blocked me. In fact being dyslexic could never block anyone, but how the mind reacts to being dyslexic could be a block.

STOP
Based on the above, what tools do you have at your disposal?
What are your limitations?

Journal..
....
....
....

You don't attract what you want. You attract what you are.
                                            - Mahatma ("Great Soul") Gandhi, 1869 - 1948

Failure = Giving up

Failure is temporary, unless you let your mind say otherwise. Failure is not fatal unless you believe that it is.

Nobody can go back and start a new beginning, but anyone can start today and make a new ending.   - Maria Robinson

What Would you Do If You Knew You Could Not Fail?

These words were planted in my mind and I knew that I had to write about the concept. To read them, you have to read my other book *Trees, the Guardians of the Soul*, a book of short spiritual and motivational stories.

STOP
What would you attempt to do if you knew that you could not fail? Write down at least six items.
---

1. ....

2. ....

3. ....

4. ....

5. ....

6. ....

What are you going to do about these? ....

....

INTROSPECTION

What is it that creates a barrier between you and success? Look at your perceptions and belief structures and see how these create obstacles.

Journal: ....

....

....

....

....

Don't Give Up

As long as your spirit is strong and you are confident, you can face anything. But if you let your spirit be crushed, you've had it. The only alternative to perseverance is failure. Perseverance is not one long race. It is many short races, one after another. Make sure that you remain firm.

Our doubts are traitors and make us lose the good we oft might win by fearing to attempt. — William Shakespeare

Mistakes

Mistakes are not failure – we learn through mistakes.

Success is achieved by understanding and understanding is achieved through acknowledging error.

You're in Financial Trouble Right Now

We have spoken about failure or mistakes as if they were in the past. This section: *You're in financial trouble right now,* is designed to help you cope if the pressure is on *right now.* Such as: the medical bills are mounting or the car is about to be repossessed. With debts like these, you are likely to feel gloom and a ball of guilt (fear) in your stomach, you'll be constantly nervous, with the worst scenarios playing out in your mind.

STOP
Take control. Take time to come back to the present moment.
Just for now let go of the worries and find yourself in this instant.
Look within to ground yourself.

....

....

....

....

Things are never as bad as they seem to be. There is a wonderful thing called time. Time helps you to solve problems. You think the car will be taken away because you did not make the payment? Well it won't, as you will still have some **time**. Take note: *all deadlines can be challenged.* Phone the car company and ask for more time. Each and every debt has a deadline and should be met with fortitude. All debts can be extended – finance companies don't want to foreclose and most will listen to you.

If you are worried about money or a situation that is developing, create a snapshot in your mind of the situation as it is right now. Then understand that there are many more snapshots (time) until the crisis is likely to occur. By doing so you have the opportunity to intervene and change the final snapshot before the problem arises.

To worry about a future event is to prepare for failure.

For you to solve your problems there has to be action, for **in action there is hope**.

While you sit and bemoan your problems, they will just get bigger and bigger until they smother you. But when you realise that, *in action there are possibilities*, mountains can be moved. It may seem hopeless but keep going, continue working towards a resolution. You have to replace the negativity with a bright smile. When you smile you remain positive. When you are positive things will get better.

Yes, be aware of your financial difficulties, but know that you can turn them around if you have the will!

No problem is so formidable that you can't walk away from it. - Charles M. Schulz

Remember to ask the Universe for help. Call it prayer if you wish. If you ask with a belief that you will be helped and if you have taken action as suggested above, you will be helped. Your debts will not be paid for by God (he is not a banker) but something will open up to help you.

To be helped by the Universe you have to be in action, for God *helps those who help themselves*. The Universe will not support you if you sit and wait for the cavalry to appear over the horizon. You have to do your bit. St James puts it: "**Faith without work is dead**". You also have to be positive. If you are negative, your vibrations will take you away from the solution (towards the right of the ego line).

When you invoke the Universe to help, do it with the conviction that provided you do your bit, the Universe will meet you halfway. You work as a team when asking for help in resolving situations. Don't ask for a fist full of bucks as you will not get them. Ask instead for guidance or openings and support.

There will be times when nothing seems to happen, but know that everything is in place and that things are going on behind the scenes. Continue being positive and carry on with action and you will get through. In time you will emerge better off than you are now.

It is fitting to finish this chapter with:

We are confronted with insurmountable opportunities.
- Walt Kelly, Pogo

Introspection = Power

You have read a good portion of this book. Are you doing the introspections given in each section? If not, then you are only intellectualising the material. To really derive the benefits, you need to internalise it and you can only do this in the lower brain waves that introspection offers.

The things you tell yourself are the things you believe

Thoughts in = Mode of Behaviour Out

You learnt from the introduction why Knowing Yourself is so important and that you have millions of thoughts per year and that most are on the same recurring themes. Like one of those old long-playing records that is stuck in the same groove, your mind is playing, *I don't trust people, I don't trust people, I don't trust people, I don't trust people, I don't trust people,* several hundred thousand times in you life. Or it could be – *I would be happy if I was in a relationship, I would be happy if I was in a relationship, I would be happy if I was in a relationship, I would be happy if I was in a relationship* and so on. Rubbish In equals Rubbish Out and so this is what becomes real for you. You believe you cannot trust, or you believe you will not be happy if you are not in a relationship.

These thoughts are mostly of a subliminal nature and play softly in the background whilst you shower, drive and during all the other activities that fill your life.

There has been a lot of research into the effects of subliminal messages and how they alter our perspective. Advertisers know this and in the 1960's used subliminal techniques to influence the public. Most countries have banned subliminal advertising. Do you know why? Because it works - but unfairly!

There are many self-help CD's that play music, but beneath the music there are empowering messages, such as, *I can give up smoking.* Because we are unconscious of our negative 'chatterbox', our subliminal programming very often disempowers us.

What is it that you tell yourself? ……………………………………………………..
………………………………………………………………………………………………
………………………………………………………………………………………………
………………………………………………………………………………………………
………………………………………………………………………………………………
……………………………………………………………………………………………
……………………………………………………………………………………………...

"As we think, so shall we be."

What you consistently think about yourself and your abilities is what you will become.

Your life will be aligned to that thought process. If you are unaware of your thoughts, you will not know if you are re-shuffling your incorrect perceptions ready to re-deal them in the same old way.

Be Aware

You know who comes into your house and who stays over. You allow nice people to linger and encourage unfriendly people to leave. If they make a mess then you clean it up. Why is your mind any different? Why let bad thoughts reside that overwhelm the good thoughts, thereby allowing mess to accumulate? As you tidy your house, so you should tidy your mind.

Thoughts Create

Thoughts will produce whatever you point them at.

They create skyscrapers and misery, they create happiness and works of art, they break marriages and make you rich or poor, healthy or sick. They give rise to a strong self-belief or place you in a position of failure. They create your friends or lack of. They are responsible for your past, your present and will shape your future.

Pure Consciousness is Neither Positive nor Negative

Painting Your Life – *The ramblings of a writer*

Our thoughts are the energy that manifests on the canvas of our lives. We're born with a clean slate but as we take control of our existence - we paint it dark, we paint it light, we paint it grim, we paint it happy. Our thoughts are the hands that direct the brush - they are the eyes that give direction, the voice that shouts the way. Gleeful feelings with trust and faith will produce a vibrant and glorious story. Gloomy thoughts direct the brush to produce a scene of holocaust.

The wonderful thing about life is that at any time we have the ability to re-paint over our work, to create those palettes of happiness and flowered forests full of joy. Stand back, look at the painting of yourself and see it for what it is. Having done so, take the time to visualise vibrant petals of love and joy. As you are your own artist, start painting now!

To cover dark with light may take a few coats, so start in one corner of your life and gradually move over your entire composition to draw in happiness, sketch wealth, mould love and sculpt health.

Anthony De Mello says, "If you are damaged, you did it; and if you are helped, you did it. If you are happy, you did it; if you are sad, you also did it."

Can you take responsibility for your damage or happiness? ....
....
....
....
....

In life, there are many things that dictated where you are today. For instance, you do not have much control over your physical appearance. Nor to a certain degree, the hand that life has dealt you. You do, however, have control over how you handle the disappointments and frustrations in life, the manner in which you respond to those situations.

Henry Ford said, "If you think you can or you can't, you're always right."

STOP
What are your prevailing negative beliefs?

Consistent negative thoughts: ....
....
....
....
....

Things are only impossible until they're not.
                -Jean-Luc Piracy, 'Star Trek: The Next Generation'

A positive attitude means enjoying what you have rather that seeing what is missing.

The only thing that you have absolute control over is your attitude!

Breaking The System

Clearly, you cannot monitor all of the thoughts that pass through your mind. But you do need to be aware of the <u>trends</u> of your thoughts and to turn the negative trends into positive ones. You can evoke an environment where the thoughts are more likely to be **positive** than **negative**. When you are able to do that you *break the system*. You can create the wonderful life that was intended for you.

Try to aim at changing what may be a mind-set that is, say, 70% negative to that of 50% positive and 50% negative. Then set your goal to get down to 40% negative and up to 60% positive. As you do this, you will see your life improving as mine did.

When you imbue your conscious and subconscious minds with positive and loving thoughts you tend to develop faith in your abilities and trust that life will be kind to you. It comes from an understanding that the Universal Spirit gives you the power to create what you want. Thoughts lead and creation follows with manifestation. Breaking the system takes you from a life that pushes you around to one where you know all things are possible.

The only way to break the system is through awareness. Awareness is left of the ego line and non-awareness is to the right.

INTROSPECTION

Relax in the normal way and consider your thoughts today. Estimate the negative to positive ratio. Negative thoughts fit into the category of 'it's a lousy day' type of statement. Then try and feel the negative thoughts as a feeling within you. Take note of these and record them when you come out. Do the same with your positive thoughts. Make sure you come out of the introspection feeling good about yourself.

Journal: ……………………………………………………………………………………
……………………………………………………………………………………………
……………………………………………………………………………………………
……………………………………………………………………………………………
……………………………………………………………………………………………

How Does it Work?

I think most readers will acknowledge that things go better when they have more of a positive mind-set than if they don't. Even knowing that, most people still remain negative.

STOP
Do you believe that life improves with a positive outlook?
If you do, why do you think this is so?
What power organises circumstances to be more favourable when you approach things positively?

....
....
....

The answer is, when you are positive you are closer to the vibration of the Universe. When you are negative your vibrations are further out of balance with the Universe. When you are in balance with the Universe you work with it and the Universe works with you. It is from this unity that all things are possible.

Albert Einstein, 1879 – 1955, thinker and scientist extraordinaire said, "There are two ways to live your life. One is as though nothing is a miracle. The other is as though everything is a miracle."

Right and Left Brain Garbage

Our brain has two hemispheres. At birth and through the influence of our environment we tend be either more right-brained (creative) or left-brained (logical). This is not fixed and we can train ourselves to be both creative and logical. We can be an artist (right-brained), but also manage a business (left- brained). We can landscape our garden and design the interior of our house (both right-brained), while at the same time design computer software (left-brained).

By believing that you are predominately right- or left-brained, you limit yourself. To expand yourself from a logical to a more creative person or vice versa, only requires awareness and confidence that you can achieve the desired result. When you do this, you will release many skills that you did not know you had.

Male - Female Energy

Another limitation is to only use our female energy if we are female or male energy if we are male. We need to be aware of our energies and develop those that we do not use. The female/male energies are opposing but complementary.

When I was brought up, the culture of the day dictated that boys and men be 'rough and tough'. So I was, and I don't know if there is anything rougher or tougher than being a 'brickie'. For years, being the stereotyped male inhibited my abilities. Only when I began getting in touch with the feminine side of my nature did my creative ability emerge. How sad it would have been to keep them suppressed. For instance, only when I recognised the feminine, did I start to write.

How many women say, "Fred looks after the finances, I could never do that"? In this case the woman thinks that business is 'men's work'. Not so, it is better for all of us to be on top of our business matters. How wonderful it is for men to cook. It is beautiful to see a woman digging in the garden and what additional compassion a father can bring to his child when he has a more balanced viewpoint.

When you develop and understand the other gender side of your psyche, you are more rounded. It gives you a whole new range of abilities and skills. You have a greater empathy for the members of the opposite sex. When I developed my feminine side, I did not become gay or effeminate. I am still very much heterosexual, yet I see things from a different perspective. I use this side of myself in business, in relationships, at almost any time. It doesn't mean that women have to become hard, as we sometimes see in company management, but it does mean that a man can express an emotion if he feels so inclined.

Why live with only 50% of your ability? Of course, when you develop the other side of your nature you move away from conforming to socially acceptable norms. You may lose some of your friends, but you will gain new buddies who, like you, will be inclined to non-conformity and are likely to be thinkers in their own right.

To develop your other side, all you have to do is develop an awareness of it and let go of your culturally-invoked beliefs. It may take you a while to let your other half emerge but the balance will be worth it.

INTROSPECTION

Make yourself comfortable and relax. If you are a man, visualise being the woman of the house. If you are a mother, see yourself as the father. Play a movie in your mind of being a parent of the opposite sex. If you are assuming the roll of the woman, adopt a bit more compassion, intuitive understanding and sensitivity towards your child. If you are role-playing the man, see yourself as not quite so emotional. Be more logical and direct.

Record your impressions: ....

....
....
....
....

Taking Responsibility for Your Thoughts

I wake up every day with the expectation that something great is going to happen. This is not in the form of money falling down the chimney. It can be something that I learn or come to understand, or perhaps a person I meet or a relationship that improves. These expectations do not necessarily arrive with a band and trumpets blaring. They can be subtle or even manifest slowly. I go to bed each night thankful for the day's blessings.

STOP
What are the thoughts that greet you each morning,
the thoughts that set your day?
Are they likely to raise your spirits or drag them down?
What are the thoughts you retire with when you climb into bed?

Journal: ....
....
....
....
....

STOP
Are you committed to retaining only positive thoughts?

Journal: ....
....
....
....
....

All the Main Religions

Certainly one of the most common precepts among all the main religions is that thoughts are creative and that we become what we think.

All things are possible to him that believeth. — Mark 9:23

As he thinketh in his heart, so is he. — Proverbs 23:7

Buddhist teachings say: "As a knight guards his castle, so one must guard one's mind from dangers outside and dangers inside; one must not neglect it for a moment." Also from the Buddha: "The mind is everything, what you think you become."

Hindu literature states: "Man becomes that of which he thinks."

Positive and Negative Vibration

Should you require proof that being positive or negative has a major effect on your physiology and success/happiness quotient, then the following section should help to convince you of the need to remain in a positive and loving state of mind as much as possible.

Everything is a vibration. Quantum physics proves that substance is nothing more than vibration. All creatures emit a consistent range of frequencies - in general; the more primitive the organism the lower the bandwidth. Advanced animals have higher frequencies. For instance, the range that an ant emits is around 1500 KHz, while a human's range starts from about 9000 KHz. For this discussion, what we are interested in is the fact that frequencies can be measured. Each human has their own unique frequency. These change according to our moods. That's why music (which is also a vibration) can change our mood. A human in a specific mood would emit a specific vibration or frequency. To recap thus far, as your mind-set changes, so does your vibrational frequency.

You may ask, "So how do I know what is a good or bad vibration?"

The answer comes from the amazing revelations of Masaru Emoto and his work on water and crystals. In his bestseller, *The Hidden Messages in Water*, he proves beyond any doubt that our moods affect our cells. Masaru is a Japanese scientist who discovered that molecules of water are affected by thought, words and feelings. Since humans (and for that matter the earth) are made up of roughly 70% water (some of our organs are up to 82% water) any changes in our body water will have a major influence on our health or success.

Masaru and his team of researchers froze water and took photos of the resulting crystal patterns. But before doing this, they offered the water with words or thoughts of either a positive or negative nature. For instance, the word 'hate' produced deformed crystal patterns, whereas words or thoughts like 'love' and 'gratitude' generated patterns as delicate and lovely as the best cut-glass or jewellery that man is capable of making. Music resulted in different crystal patterns. Soft and gentle sounds offered the most beautiful patterns, whilst heavy metal fragmented the patterns.

As his work developed he learnt that water expresses itself in a vast variety of ways that are consistent with the medium fed to it - clearly water has intelligence. Emoto says, "To understand water is to understand the very cosmos and life itself."

When I read his work I realised that he had discovered the most profound truths and was further proof that our thoughts influence our very being right down to a cellular level. The impact that love and gratitude have on water, and therefore on us and the world beyond ourselves, is a major breakthrough in the development of mankind. Words and thought flow from an intent. That intent results in a vibration. Water on its own does not change anything, it is merely an intelligent medium that mirrors our internal state or that of the planet. Our collective vibration is a result of our collective thought. The condition of the world is a direct result of our collective consciousness.

But lets return to the matter at hand – you. Motivational teachers as well as spiritual masters have been telling us for hundreds of years just how important it is to remain positive and loving. Emoto's work, coupled with the understanding of how vibrations function, is all the proof that any rational human would need to understand the importance of remaining positive and loving.

To recap, everything is a vibration and we can measure those vibrations. Thoughts (as seen through Emoto's work) create higher or lower vibrations as a result of what we think.

AFFIRMATIONS AND VISUALISATIONS

Continuing The Thought Process, our minds are bombarded with thousands of thoughts daily. Trying to keep track and in control of them is impossible. We can, nevertheless, direct the thoughts that have the greatest influence over our lives. We do this with awareness, and with a formal practice of affirmations and visualisations. It is a period of slowing the mind down and dedicating it to the creating of positive thoughts.

Monitoring your thoughts

Although most people know that a positive mind-frame leads to a better life, most don't manage it. The reason is, it is difficult to remember to monitor your mind. The mind is like a television that plays in the background. On and on it goes without consciousness or awareness. It is the awareness that we need to have. But as I said, it is difficult. That is why it is so important to have periods of positive thinking which include affirmations and visualisations.

Affirmations and visualisations work hand-in-hand with each other. Visualisations show, whilst affirmations tell the mind. Remember what was said earlier about subliminal messages? Affirmations are your own subliminal method for nourishing your mind with empowering messages.

Positive affirmations and visualisation help reverse the years of negative self-programming and establish a positive state of mind.

Affirmations, especially when expressed with belief, flow into the unconscious mind, aligning it with the conscious one.

Negative Affirmations

Most people unknowingly use affirmations, but in a negative way, i.e. 'I'm no good at making speeches'. Through negative affirmations we are brainwashed into sickness, money problems, relationship issues and unwanted modes of behaviour. The longer we have been in a negative state, the greater we will need to use affirmations to reverse the negative influence.

What are your negative thoughts? ....

....

....

....

What negative thoughts did you have today? ....

....

....

....

....

How To Use Affirmations

For affirmations to work, they need to be in the first person and in the present moment. They work better if done on a consistent basis. The more you connect to your feelings and the more power you give your affirmations, the greater will be your success.

When visualising or verbalising do not use negative words or thoughts.

Remember Matthew 21:22 states quite clearly that, "Believing, you will receive."

Therefore, you must believe in yourself and your affirmations. The visualisations must reflect this belief.

It is always best to create your own affirmations to invoke your desire.

Do you think that you will receive if you believe? ....

....

....

....

INTROSPECTION

Choose a goal that you would like to achieve. For ten minutes see it happening in your mind while saying, "I am powerful beyond measure and I am.......................... (e.g. the owner of a brand new house). Say it aloud and feel it.

It may be difficult to visualise and speak at the same time, while keeping invading thoughts at bay. You'll improve with practise and no effort will be wasted.

Using Affirmations and Visualisations Together to Gain Clarity

Another benefit of visualisations and affirmations is the collation of your concepts. Your thoughts are usually scattered and so you need methods to:

- Clarify
- Understand
- Align/focus
- Enthuse

Vision

Manifestation starts with a connection to Source, and is compounded with affirmation and belief. You reduce or improve your ability in direct proportion to your vision.

Another word for vision is imagination. Imagination is a wonderful skill. It is a weapon against mediocrity and a tool for growth. Imagination can elevate you to a better position in life. A lack of imagination will stifle your potential. In fact, without imagination you have no potential.

You have either imagination or complacency. They are at odds with one another. It is you who writes the script and decides which one will be most prominent.

It is necessary to hold before you what you want to become or achieve. Affirmations help you do this. It is advisable to repeat your wishes and desires daily, to have them ever present in your consciousness.

Knowing It Is So Before Achieving It

When you do your visualisation and affirmations, it is important to know it and internalise it, even though you are not (yet) it. If you don't believe that you already are something or have something, your mind will believe that the 'something' will only happen in the future. You will continually be chasing a future goal. Be it now, to become it later!

This may sound false, but Aristotle was aware of the value of *be it now to become it later* when he said – **"For the things we have to learn, before we can do them, we learn by doing them."**

"The way to gain a good reputation is to endeavour to be what you desire to appear." - Socrates (Philosopher c 469 – 399 BC)

Visualisations help you to maintain the goals of your desires. When you are able to live it, then it is more likely that you will attain it. Visualisation keeps the dream alive. Visualisation maintains the belief that you are able to manifest what you set out to achieve. By visualising you are able to make the abstract real, to give it a life.

In the early days of Walt Disney, everyone thought that he was 'wacky'. Yet Disneyland became the reality of his imagination and visualisations. Walt was a visionary. You too are a visionary. You just may not know it yet.

I used to run a lot of road races and to improve speed I read many books on training principles. One such book related a story about how one of the top track runners from the collegial circuit in America developed an injury six weeks before a major meeting. For five of those weeks he couldn't train. Everyone thought he would pull out. He didn't and went on to win the race. How did he do this? Everyday he did introspections where he visualised training and also the race. For a thirty-minute period each day he relaxed and focused his mind on the outcome he wanted. In his mind he ran every step of the track as if it was real. During the meditations, he was it and so he became it. He used all of his senses so that he could hear the gun going off and crowd shouting, the colours of the track and the athletes. He felt the pushing and shoving that goes on in those races and of course the tape as he crossed the line.

ABUNDANCE = Your Birth right

Abundance means, to flow with love, joy, happiness, prosperity, success, vitality, laughter, generosity and all the good things in life. There is more than enough of everything for all, which does not only mean wealth. If you claim your abundance, you will never be separated from it. The Supreme Being gave you the choice to allow you to either create or dissipate your own abundance.

How many times have you been in financial binds, where there have seemingly been dead-end roads? Yet somehow, you scrape through. It is interesting to note that people who live on a breadline can usually manifest extras for emergencies. This would indicate that the only thing keeping them on a month-to-month tightrope is their own lack of manifestation. They always seem to have the solution to just scrape through! Money (which is only energy) seems to arrive when it is needed most.

If this is the case, why do we not manifest more money? Instead of manifesting to just get by, we can manifest to line our nests with all the good things we deserve.

Manifesting your abundance is a contract between yourself and The Divine. Your side of the bargain is to believe in yourself and have faith. You also have to work towards positive outcomes. The Divine's side of the agreement flows naturally to your aid once you fulfil your side of the bargain. When you obey your side of the deal, you align yourself with the energy of The Creator.

If you count your blessings and not your troubles you will move closer to the alignment of what was suggested above.

Abundance will only manifest when you have a connection to Source, or a connection to Source will facilitate you abundance.

And what do I mean by connection?

Connection is a conscious awareness that you are one with all. It is a conscious awareness of being the light and love. This conscious awareness must be in the present moment and as often as possible – when having breakfast, driving to work, when at work.

If there is no connection, no conscious awareness, there will be no abundance.

As you are part of the Oneness, you do not need to look outside of yourself, you need to look within. If you look outside of yourself, you create a division or duality from Source, the Oneness.

Full connection takes you beyond your fears (as if you are in fear you will not connect); it will take you beyond pettiness and negativity. It is from this platform that your abundance and manifestation will start to flow.

The same Provide(nce) that sustains "the birds of heaven and the flowers of the field will sustain you." — Matthew 6:26-30

> **STOP**
> **Do you believe that last quotation?**
> **If so, then your direction is clear.**

Journal: ....
....
....
....
....

Abundance and Separation

Illness is a separation from health, unhappiness is separation from harmony, poverty is separation from substance, anger is separation from love.

Previously, in the section about ego, you learned that ego or negativity was to the right of the ego line. So too are separations to the right of the line. Negativity separates you from health. Negativity separates you from happiness, wealth and love.

FORGIVING

What is forgiveness?

My dictionary describes it as 'a remit, a let off, a pardoning of offenders. It is a cessation of blame.' It is interesting to note that the next word in the same dictionary is FORGO, which is to give up.

Forgiveness - Man's Hardest Lesson

I believe that forgiveness is one of man's greatest and hardest lessons. As you will see from these writings, there is much to understand about forgiveness. There is love, compassion, honesty, strength of character, understanding, tolerance and a willingness to put aside our ego and our pain. Forgiveness is not a passive action. It takes a conscious decision, an act of will. This perhaps is stating the obvious, but the obvious needs to be emphasised.

Forgiveness is one of the major cornerstones of leading a fulfilling and spiritual life. This is why it is imperative that you understand forgiveness and apply the principles. It is a long section but full of advice.

Often when people forgive, they do so superficially. They may have said the words but retain anger, resentment and hang-ups. They may say they forgive because it is expedient to do so – to allow an argument to subside. Yet the so-called forgiver is still very angry.

For this discussion I am going to introduce a concept of **real forgiveness**, i.e. forgiveness from where you are so clear of the anger or hurt that you have no grudge or axe to grind. <u>Your acceptance is so complete, you don't even feel that there is a need to forgive</u>. This is the operative state of mind. This is to the left of the ego line.

STOP
Do you agree that forgiveness is man's hardest lesson?

Journal: ....

....

....

....

....

And can you have total acceptance? ....

....

....

....

....

I have read that in many instances of physiological complaints, resentment is part of the case history. Bad will and grudges cause dis-ease in the body. It is forgiving and not medication that will heal. Only we can cure our 'grudgitis'.

If you are serious about overcoming your inadequacies, then it is important to remove all resentment from within. You must be determined as it may not be easy to do this. For some, it requires lots of hard work.

Also understand that you will not be spiritually blessed until you learn to forgive.

Blood stains cannot be removed by more blood; resentment cannot be removed by more resentment. Resentment can be removed only by forgetting it. — Buddha

Forgiving and Love

The link between forgiving and a loving nature cannot be underestimated. To forgive with **real forgiveness** we need love. If we love ourselves and are filled with love for life, we are more likely to be able to grant **real forgiveness**.

Forgiveness is an expression of love based on acceptance. Accepting does not mean that we have to like it. It means we are willing to let it go.

When you are serious about forgiving, you have to dredge out the anger. But like a hole in the sand, it will keep filling up with hate and resentment. That is unless you swap it with something else. Ensure that you replace it with love.

There is nothing stronger than gentleness.
— Han Suyin, *Forgiving and the Great Religions*

The KJ V: 01 Bible discusses the absolute necessity of living life with a forgiving nature. To get the message across, it discusses forgiveness **fifty-three** times.

From Buddhism: "Never is hate diminished by hatred. It is only diminished by love."

Conquer your foe by force and you increase his anger, conquer by love and you will reap no sorrow. — Unknown

"When righteousness is practised to win peace, he who so walks shall gain the victory and all fetters utterly destroy."
— Unknown

Hinduism – "The noble-minded dedicate themselves to the promotion of peace and the happiness of others; even those who injure them."

Islam – "Forgive thy servant seventy times a day."

Judaism – "The most beautiful thing a man can do is to forgive wrong."

An ancient Chinese proverb tells us, "The one who pursues revenge should dig two graves."

Forgiving and Self-Worth

When you have self-worth (or love yourself) you naturally have a generous demeanour from which you are able to forgive. If your love for yourself is limited, it is unlikely that you will find the love for **real forgiveness**.

'Self-worth' or lack of it is usually about being unable to receive love. When you forgive, you create space for love to flow back to you. People with self-esteem issues cannot receive love or blessings from others. So guess what? They will not forgive. Their belief is that they do not deserve the return of love that comes from forgiveness.

Can you receive love from strangers? ....
....
....
....

Forgiving and Being Right (or maintaining guilt)

There are times when someone may not forgive you. They prefer to keep you a prisoner of guilt or to prove themselves to be right. The longer they justify themselves in their position of "I am correct in this issue" and project guilt on to you, the more they morally 'justify' their position. They say to themselves, "Look how angry you made me, I must be right", which becomes a form of control over you.

> **STOP**
> **Have you ever done this or had it done to you?**
> **I am sure you have.**

Journal: ....
....
....
....
....

There will be times, especially in a relationship, when one party supposedly 'damages' the other. The damaged person may extract as much mileage as possible from the perpetrator, until they are *finally* ready to forgive. They will ensure the perpetrator feels guilty for their misdemeanour for as long as possible. They will remain the victim until they feel that they have suitably chastised and gained the upper hand. These people delude themselves. They remain in the past and retain unnecessary anger and resentment.

Look very closely at yourself. Are you this type of person? Review your past arguments and analyse your behaviour. If you have this trait, look at what you have to gain from the way you behave and the reasons for it. In this case the person is trying to make him or her self correct and you wrong. These tactics work on those individuals who are weak enough to accept them (victims).

Forgiving and Fear

Many people operate from a position of fear. If you are this type of person, you have to be scrupulously honest with yourself. If you are fear-based, it is unlikely that you will be able to forgive easily as the self-assurance required for forgiveness will be absent. Fear-based people operate from the same position as people with limited self-esteem.

When you are unable to forgive, you need to be able to identify that child within you who will not let go.

Forgiving and Apologising

A person who is unable to apologise is normally unable to forgive. In both instances, there needs to be a healthy level of honesty with oneself. For instance, people who say things that are meant to hurt, but don't take ownership by apologising, are also the people who will not forgive you for your behaviour.

Sorry seems to be the hardest word. — Elton John

Forgiveness and Lessons in Life

Carrying grudges is a great way to give away your power and insert blockages. Until you learn to forgive, circumstances that require forgiveness will keep appearing in your life. In other words, forgiving is an experience to overcome. These continuous lessons will not be fun. In fact they will be painful. When you cannot forgive you will be stuck and unable to grow or move forward until you become un-stuck. You will probably become un-stuck only as a result of the constant barrage of incidents that require **real forgiving**. In the end you will see that there is no alternative but to look at things differently.

A Course in Miracles teaches that forgiveness is unknown in Heaven. There is no need for it. If you give no life to it – there is nothing to forgive.

Forgiving and Compassion

To forgive someone with **real forgiveness** requires compassion. If compassion is missing then tolerance and understanding will not be there. A lack of compassion indicates lack of conscience.

Forgiving and Moving On

Revenge, anger, hate and retaliation are all debilitating actions that hinder you from living a happy and stress-free life. **Many people would rather be right than be happy!**

When you do not forgive a person or situation, you are bound to that person or issue. Unresolved processes generate bad feelings and resentment, therefore you remain stuck. You can never be positive if you harbour hate, bitterness, anger or resentment.

Our anger does not affect the people who hurt us. It only hurts us. — Unknown

Whisper words of wisdom, let it be. — *Paul McCartney*

Forgiving and Releasing Anger

It is amazing how good you feel after offering **real forgiveness** to someone. You may have carried bitterness around with you for months but the minute you say and mean 'I forgive you' the bitterness disappears.

When you forgive, you in no way change the past, but you sure do change the future.
— *Bernard Meltzer, Forgiving and Judgement*

When we are unable to forgive, we are in a state of judgement. The next topic on judgemental behaviour explains how judgement carries emotion. Furthermore, we do not have the right to judge anyone. If anyone has seemingly done us harm, let life be the arbitrator and karma the punishment. Our job is to learn, forgive and move on.

STOP
Are you judgemental about an issue at the moment?

Journal: ....
....
....
....

Forgiving Acts of Violence Against Us

How do you forgive those who have physically degraded you? Well, the process is linked with healing. If you don't forgive you'll not heal. The minute you make the decision to heal you move towards forgiveness. The minute you decide to forgive you move towards healing. You have to make those decisions simultaneously. You have to bring in love, trust and a willingness to let go. Only then will the body of anger dissolve.

To help in the healing/forgiveness process, use introspection. The more you can go inside with love and compassion the faster the healing/forgiveness process will be.

Fortunately I have never been in a situation where one person fully degraded me. And for this discussion, clearly, I am not in a position to know how it feels. But I do know that if the hurt is so bad, forgiveness may be intolerable and that's when it is needed the most. But if you can't forgive, then at least try to let go and move along. Don't remain in that hurt. Strive for something more positive. When you move on you can gain the space that may allow you to consider forgiveness. But remember the longer you delay that forgiveness, the slower your recovery will be. *In action there is hope.*

Lewis B. Smedes taught: "When we forgive evil we do not excuse it, we do not tolerate it, we do not smother it. We look the evil full in the face, call it what it is, let its horror shock and stun and enrage us, and only then do we forgive it."

Also by B Smedes, "Forgiving does not erase the bitter past. A healed memory is not a deleted memory. Instead, forgiving what we cannot forget creates a new way to remember. We change the memory of our past into a hope for our future."

It may seem harsh that there is a reason for everything that ever happened to you. **In God's work there is no wastage.** There is not too much water on the planet or too many trees. We don't suffocate because there is a surplus of oxygen. The act of violence that may have been committed against you, as twisted as it may seem, may also not be wasted – perhaps it is your greatest teacher.

STOP
Seriously consider that the act of violence that may have been committed against you may also be your teacher!

Journal: ....
....
....
....
....
....

To forgive is to Understand
To move towards **real forgiveness** requires empathy to understand the other person or situation. From understanding comes allowance for the humanness of situations, which helps us to develop compassion.

You will only be able to understand the person or situation if you are willing to put aside anger and resentment. You will not allow yourself to comprehend things clearly if you are beset by emotion. When you perceive situations in a balanced, mature way, it makes it easier to remove the sting. But you have to be willing.

To forgive yourself you must first understand yourself. If you have not forgiven yourself, you need to introspect fully on every aspect of the issue. From this you can create a list of items you are grieving about. Then you can release that issue. If you do not consciously know what the issue is you can't release it.

The same applies to forgiving someone else. Determine clearly the reasons for your anger and resentment. Create a list and release each item in turn.

Forgiving Thyself

No section on forgiveness would be complete without a discussion on forgiving ThySelf. Sometimes we do things we are not proud of or feel guilty about. When we make mistakes we deride and berate ourselves and feel guilty.

There are times when circumstances may be beyond our control but we blame ourselves anyway. When these things happen, we can either wallow in self pity or we can forgive ourselves and move on. We need to look (introspect) at what we did or didn't do and look at it from a point of view of understanding. We need to tell ourselves that it is OK to make mistakes. Remember mistakes can lead to growth and wisdom. We need to apologise to the people we hurt and then set about forgiving ourselves and releasing it. We need to accept with total compassion and not be hard on ourselves.

> **STOP**
> **Look for a time in your life where you felt guilty or were hard on yourself. In your introspection focus on that time and watch it melt like a piece of ice.**

Journal notes: ....
....
....
....
....

Real Forgiving Takes Time

In order to forgive yourself or someone else you will have to work on yourself for a while before you are ready to let go. It is unlikely that you will be able to forget the resentment or anger by just saying "I forgive you" or "I forgive myself". Usually forgiveness is not instantaneous, it takes time. Do this by consciously thinking of the person and forgiving them with love. Each time you do this you will find that there is a little less hurt. Your thoughts need to be proactive.

Sometimes it helps to write a 'good-will' letter to the person you know you must forgive. Put down all the good that that person has within. When finished, you need not send it, as you are simply helping to release your anger. Letters of this nature have a rejuvenating and healing affect. They also require clarity and perception of thought. Clarity can be gained merely through the writing.

Love is light; unforgiving is dark. Turn on the light.
- Unknown

Snapshot - *Dad again*

I think that it was Keith, my elder brother, who brought the kitten home. I must have been about ten at the time. It was tiny, only about four-weeks old and was jet black. John, Keith and I instantly loved it and kept it hidden from Dad, who didn't like cats. For two weeks we kept it a secret but Dad eventually found it. After the lecture on the evils of cats, he grabbed it and told us to, "Come." He drove us to the local rubbish dump, some five or six kilometres away and ditched it. Then rubbing his hands together in a manner of – now that was easy enough, said, "No more cat". We were devastated as we drove away, leaving a forlorn Kitty on top of a pile of junk.

The story does not end here, as about ten days later, Kitty, like a homing pigeon, somehow found his way back. This was truly miraculous and defies logic, yet there he was. We did not even have time to fatten him up, when again he was discovered by Dad. Rolling his sleeves up he said, "I will now do the job properly." He got a bag out of the shed and put a brick and kitty into it and tied the top. We were told, "Stay here," as he and the bag drove towards the beach. Upon his return he told us with glee that he had thrown the bag with the brick and kitty into the ocean.

Poor Kitty, even he could not Houdini his way out of that one. We were broken and it took a long time before we would speak to Dad again. And certainly we would not bring any more cats home, as we were too petrified Dad would find out.

Although I do not condone Dad's behaviour, I have forgiven him and now hold no anger for his actions. I also understand that he is on his own journey and has his own lessons to learn. There is good in everybody, but everybody does bad things from time to time. There is much good in my Dad, but I report on his actions merely to show you what shaped my thought processes about forgiveness.

All things are beautiful, but it is man that clouds the vision by giving out hate and anger. An uncompromising attitude perpetuates these emotions. Forgiveness, on the other hand, reduces negative emotions.

Why is it so hard to forgive? Why can't you just let go? To answer this, go back to the section on ego. ....
....
....

Forgiveness must come from the heart. Otherwise it is not forgiveness.

"How do we heal our wounds – starve them. Stop speaking about them and make this day the day to be remembered."
-Ansi Du Plessis, (teacher and healer)

Nelson Mandela - A wonderful act of forgiveness

Nelson Mandela was incarcerated in a South African jail for 27 years, sometimes in appalling conditions. He saw friends murdered and beaten. His marriage was effectively destroyed. All his life he witnessed and felt the injustices of apartheid. Yet this man forgave all. Whilst in jail he preached forgiveness. He encouraged his fellow Africans to also forgive. We, in our small ways, must emulate these large acts!

Forgiving and what you get back

If it is true that what you put out you get back, then by forgiving, you are likely to receive compassion and love in return.

Forgiving is Oneness

Forgiving is a "oneness" principle. There can be no connection to the Source without it.

Summary of Forgiving

As can be seen from the above, there is more to forgiving than one would assume.

'By forgiving or not forgiving, you learn who you really are'

INTROSPECTION

Prepare yourself and introspect on who or what you need to forgive. Then see yourself in a state of forgiveness. Encasing yourself in compassion for that issue.
Journal: ....

....
....
....
....

Try to do the above introspection several times.

GUILT

Guilt is a useless emotion as you cannot change anything you have done in your past. The best way to avoid guilt in the future is to be conscious of your actions in the present moment. If you carry guilt around as part of your 'baggage', then you need to apply forgiveness to the situation, forgive yourself and move on.

If you can physically set right a past misdemeanour, then make that phone call or write that letter of apology. It's never too late to apologise. Set yourself free and drop your feelings of guilt in the rubbish bin where they belong.

Remember that your moral code is set by you and not by society's code of ethics or that of religious institutions. If something feels right to you, there is never any reason for you to feel guilty about it.

Justifying and action

If you find yourself weighing up the moral pros and cons of an action that you consider taking, then it is probably wrong. If you feel doubtful but you want to do it anyway, then you are likely to look for supporting arguments as to why it's OK to do it.

When it comes to these decisions, if it feels right it probably is right. If it feels wrong then it probably is wrong. Use your intuition. What do your immediate thoughts say? That little voice (it may be little but it says mammoth things) inside of you is a tap into your higher self, which knows better than your conscious self.

Another way to describe your intuition is your gut feeling. Take the time to feel what your gut is telling you. For me the feeling is very real and reliable. If for instance, I say something to someone and what I say is unfair, my gut-feeling kicks in and makes me aware that I have done wrong. It is so strong that it will not leave me until I have done something about it, such as apologise.

Judgement and Observation

What is the difference between judgement and observation? Nothing except the emotion we bring to it.

Observation is necessary for without it there is ignorance. If we walk around with blinkers on, we may find ourselves in many compromising situations.

Observation is paying the necessary attention to the world and people around you. It is taking responsibility for your life. It is the opposite of the 'head in the sand' scenario.

Be non-judgemental, be cautious with criticism and be generous with praise.

Deal with the faults of others as gently as with your own.
— Chinese proverb

Self Judgement

Another aspect of judgement is self-judgement.

Derogatory self-judgement contributes directly to lack of self-esteem.

Complaining = Giving your power away

Complaining, whingeing, moaning and whining are all useless activities and behavioural traits that keep you from living your life effectively. Recognise them and drop them.

Complaining encourages self-pity. By complaining you effectively announce to the rest of the world that you are a *victim*.
Complaining is invariably a habit and as such needs to be broken.

If you find that you are a regular complainer, look at the reasons why and acknowledge them. It is only when you recognise and eradicate this debilitating *giving-away-power* activity that you move to a more positive frame of mind.

I keep returning to the need to Know ThySelf. If you do not know yourself, you won't know how much your complaining annoys and bores all who are unfortunate enough to have to listen to you. Remember, what you give out you get back – you put out 'moan', you get back reasons to moan.

STOP
What have you complained about today?
If you did moan was it absolutely necessary?
Be responsible for who you are, what you think and what you say.

Journal: ....
....
....
....
Are you a serial complainer? ....
....
....

More often than not, complainers are also judgmental.

Is your life so boring that you must constantly look for fulfilment in degrading others?

Resolve just for today that you will not complain once. The queue in the shopping centre will not worry you, nor will the fact that the last packet of XYZ was sold to the customer before you. You will not complain when the price of petrol increases. Just for today you will not moan if it is raining. Promise yourself that you will see the entire day in the best light possible.

I suggest that you make a note to remind yourself to record how much of the day you spent complaining. Do this on a daily basis, one day at a time, and watch how your friends around you change. They will moan and groan less. You will attract new and enthusiastic people into your life. By not moaning you will move to a more positive state of peace.

> **STOP**
> **Who did you hear moan today? Boring wasn't it?**

Journal notes: ....
....
....
....
....
....

COURAGE = Standing up for what you believe in, regardless of the odds against you.

You are always in a state of flux and cannot always remain on the peaks of life. There will be valleys. It takes strong legs to climb the peaks and it will take a strong character to climb from the low to the high points in life.

The only thing we have to fear is fear itself.
  — Franklin D Roosevelt, 1882-1945 (American President)

So often, it is focusing on the debilitation that fear produces which reduces us to something weaker than what we are. Take courage and half the fear will disappear.

Courage is faith and strength combined.
  — Ansi du Plessis, Teacher and healer

The main fear that holds people back is the fear of failure.

Life shrinks or expands in proportion to one's courage.
  — Anaïs Nin

STOP
Think for a minute about this last quotation.
Are your ideals governed by fears? If so, your advancement in life will be curtailed as a result of those fears.
When did fear stop you from achieving a goal?

Journal: ....
....
....
....
....

Snapshot - *School*

*I remember the fear I carried when I was in school. The worst was at exam time as exams terrified me. To my way of thinking they were not a gauge of progress, but a measure against classmates. Being dyslexic set up the most profound negativity within me. The fear of failure was so strong that I could not help myself from failing. I gave up all hope, did not study and fooled myself that I didn't care what happened. I was **back to being governed by my fear**.*

*Fortunately, years later, when evaluating myself, I was able to take faith and courage from what I had learnt about my self. From there I was able to grow to the point where I can **now achieve according to my hopes**.*

INTROSPECTION

Is there a current issue in your life where you need courage? Take the time to reflect on the issue and get a sense of how you feel about it. Take note of what anxiety feels like for you. If you don't have a current example, go into introspection and imagine a time in the past where you were fearful. Because you created the anxiety, you can also diminish it. But while you are in that space, contemplate being strong and overcoming the obstacle, then look at how you feel. There is likely to be a difference.

Did you feel the need for courage? ………………………………………………………..

……………………………………………………………………………………………………

……………………………………………………………………………………………………

……………………………………………………………………………………………………

……………………………………………………………………………………………………

Did you feel any anxiety? ……………………………………………………………………

……………………………………………………………………………………………………

……………………………………………………………………………………………………

……………………………………………………………………………………………………

……………………………………………………………………………………………………

You do not need to look for courage, it is within you, waiting to be called upon. And if you do bring it out, all types of assistance will be there to rally around you, helping you win the day.

Courage comes in many forms and you need to know when to bring it into your life. As a person of vision you will require the courage of your convictions. When experiencing a rough patch, call forth your courage with fortitude.

If you decide to quit your job to follow your dreams, you will need strength of character. To win the race takes guts, to be the best you can be requires courage. You will be required to be fearless when scraping away the muck of your life, while getting to Know ThySelf. Being totally honest with oneself is a courageous action.

There is an ancient saying; **this too shall pass**. These wonderful words can help you in times of trouble or doubt. When things seem to be against you, remember the words, **this too will pass away**. Words like these inspire us to go forward with courage. At the end of every dark night, there is the light of day.

No pain lasts forever. With courage your healing will be accelerated.

You have a problem? Accept it. Acceptance takes courage, which is the first step to resolution.

I thank God for my handicaps, for, through them, I have found my self, my work and my God.
  — Helen Keller, a blind, deaf and dumb, teacher and writer

FAMILY

What makes life worthwhile? Love does. How better to give and receive love than through your family? Deep and lasting satisfaction is not about business or how much money you have. It's not about material success. It's about mothers, fathers, wives, husbands, sons, daughters, brothers and sisters. It is giving and receiving support. It is being a part of something that is the foundation of humanity. There is nothing like the support received from a loved one. Being part of a loving family somehow makes it easier to cope with our daily lives. Be thankful and appreciative of your family.

Your family is most important. Make sure that every so often your family comes under your internal spotlight. When you internalise love and encourage your children this will become evident in your daily interaction with them. The same applies to your spouse or partner. Spend time looking at all their good points. Try and understand what you consider to be their weak points and soften your approach to them. Re-live in your mind some of the enjoyable times you have had together. Count your blessings. See yourself as being loved and respected by your family.

From time to time there will be issues. Reflect on these and work out the best course of action. Know the beauty and value of your loved ones and be aware that life is short. Do not waste time on petty squabbles. Be a pillar of strength.

Never be negative because of other people. Evaluate the character of each member and treat each as an individual.

> **STOP**
> **A dysfunctional family life is an indication of a life that does not work. Is yours functional?**

Journal: ....
....
....
....
....

Snapshot - Age 2.5 to 14 - *Dad Again*

Although I know differently now, as a kid growing up it seemed to me that Dad did not care much about us. If he did, he didn't show it and if he had emotions, then he was unable to display them. I don't ever remember being held by him, nor did he ever kiss us. We used to get handshakes. These are OK, but don't suffice for affection and certainly not love.

I remember on one of those rare outings that he took us on, I dived off a rock into water that was too shallow. My right thigh scraped along a bed of razor sharp oysters. The cuts that resulted were half the length of my thigh and the scars are still visible all these years later. It bled a lot and was painful. Yet, all Dad could say was, "That'll teach you to be careful where you dive." He was so callous and distant.

Each morning, he would be off to work just before we woke up for school. At a quarter past six in the evening, we would hear his car changing down gear and turn the corner into our driveway. He would come in and say, "How are you," but without waiting to hear the answer, would lock himself in the bathroom where he washed (I never saw my dad naked). When he emerged he would listen to the news - we had to be quiet. Then out would come the newspaper. All the time we were shut out. Dinner was had with him listening to the radio or watching television.

When we went to bed, it was the handshake, with no sharing of himself or interest in us. If throughout the evening he did say something it was invariably to moan.

The next morning he would be off to work again and the cycle continued. On weekends, he would be drunk a fair amount of the time and still be stranger-like.

He was so disinterested in us kids, not once did he ever ask us about our schooling, friends or anything that affected our lives. It was as if we had no lives.

We lived across the road from sporting grounds. In summer we played cricket and in winter it was soccer. Out of literally hundreds of games that I played there, there was only one day, just one, when Dad roused himself out of his lounge chair to cross the road and watch me play soccer. He watched half the game and re-crossed the road and went back to his couch, television and beer. When I came home several hours later, he told me what a useless player I was. At the time, I was glad that was the only time he had come to watch.

As an adult, I can understand some of the reasons why Dad was cold and distant, but at the time, when I needed his love and approval, it was not there.

He had his own demons; he had been in the German army and found himself at Stalingrad in Russia. I won't go into the details, but for those who don't know about that campaign, 300,000 German troops died and only 6,000 escaped. Many of the troops starved or froze to death in that terrible Russian winter. I don't know how Dad managed to survive, as he is so fraught with emotion that he has never spoken about that time. So, Dad, you are excused for the demons. I understand your sadness and hurt, but as a tiny tot I would have loved it if you showed some attention and played and tumbled with us - as I played and tumbled with my kids.

As you develop yourself and grow in love, compassion and patience as taught in this workbook, you will have gained 'spiritual tools' that will keep you achieve a better state of balance. My dad did not have any 'spiritual tools' and so was ill- equipped to handle the emotional hardships that he endured. After the war, how could he not smoulder with anger or be emotionally compromised? This book will help you move beyond negative conditions. Dad never had the luxury of this type of teaching.

Before Captain Scott of the Antarctic died, he had lots of time to reflect on the values of life. Apparently the last words that he wrote were "**For God's sake, look after our people**". He realised that what really matters to man is family.

I am not saying you have to have a family to be happy or have meaning in life. I am suggesting however, that a family can be the cherry on top, the added meaning. In a family unit you have a greater opportunity to express your love and you are more likely to have love expressed to you.

Recently, I went on holiday with a friend to his family farm. His mother was dying of cancer. She was very religious and told me that she knew that when she passed on Jesus would be there to lead her. Her faith allowed her to go with grace and contentment. But still, she clung to life. She hung on because of her family, not because she was worried about them. She knew that they would all be fine when her time came. She hung on because the love she had for them made hanging on worth it - even amidst all the pain. She has now gone, but the memory of the love she expressed to her family is her legacy.

That love, which was instilled in the memory of her loved ones will grow and in turn be expressed to other loved ones as time passes.

Being part of a family can be challenging at times as lessons arrive to be taught or learnt. Regard the challenges as a part of your growth.

Mid pleasures and places though we may roam, be it ever so humble, there's no place like home. — John Howard Payne

Snapshot - *A wonderful family*

Although it may seem that my life was one of hardship, it wasn't. After the orphanage we were a regular family – Mum (Enid), Dad, Keith, John and myself. Keith you may ask, who is he?

Keith was Mum's son from her first marriage. He is four and a half years older than me and at the time seemed big and sophisticated. And then, several years later, Steve came along as a result of the union between Mum and Dad.

As a family we were happy and there was never any tension between any of the members. Well, other than between Mum and Dad as they were totally different. Mum had strong feelings for Dad but she may not have married him if it was not for the plight John and I found ourselves in on the farm. Anyway, when I was about eighteen, after many years of arguing, my parents finally broke up. As it turned out, it was the best thing for both of them as they both met and married partners who they were better suited to.

To continue, we were a happy and cohesive family, Mum loved us all passionately and had the ability to make each one of us feel special. Dad on the other hand, took Keith in as his own and was relatively good to him. I say relatively, as Dad was very difficult.

We were impoverished, but comfortable. Mum and Dad both worked hard but when not working they were at home and so we saw lots of them. I have many good memories.

INTROSPECTION

Take some time to evaluate your family. If there are resentments, put them aside for the moment. Focus only on the value and what you can bring to the family in terms of love and support, remembering that you get back what you give out.

Do you have resentments? ....
....
....
....

....
....

GENEROSITY = Self love

Generosity comes in many forms, but the form referred to here is generosity of spirit - a generous and open nature.

We live in times where there are many beggars, especially in South Africa. These beggars are great at placing themselves in front of us on our path. Beggars challenge us and our attitudes and by doing so evoke all sorts of emotions, such as: guilt, revulsion or if we are lucky, compassion. Next time you are confronted by a beggar, look at your feelings. Understand why you feel the way you do. Accept your feelings but certainly know where they come from. If your feelings are negative, revise them.

A lot of people give loose change to beggars but they do so out of guilt. When this is the case, they have a lot of work to do on themselves. Giving must come from the heart, not from guilt. If it comes from guilt or fear, there is no real value in giving. In fact the beggar will feel the negativity.

As a sideline to this discussion, have you ever spoken to a street person? A person who has no possessions and has been on the street for several years? Who has no family help or does not know where his/her next meal is to come from? A person who is out in the cold in winter and the rain when it comes. You will be amazed at what you can learn. Talk to them, don't shun them, and you will get an inkling of how complex we make our lives and how the simple things can thrill you.

> **STOP**
> **Why do you think there is a chapter on generosity**
> **in this book Know Thyself?**
> **Write down your thoughts on this and look again at this question**
> **when you have finished the chapter.**

....
....
....
....

Roy, a friend of mine, has a code that he lives by. He wants to help someone in some way each and every day. There was a stage in the early days of my business when I was struggling financially. Roy heard about this and without being asked offered to lend me money. But there was one proviso - that I did not pay him any interest when I returned the money. His logic was that if he received interest, then he was gaining personally and therefore not helping in the true sense of the word.

Years later, Roy is married to a beautiful and wonderful lady. He has lovely children and is wealthy. By reading the following you will see why Roy has the bounties of life.

> May it be, O Lord, that I seek not so much to be consoled as to console, to be understood as to understand, to be loved as to love, because it is in giving oneself that one receives; it is in forgetting oneself that one is found; it is in pardoning that one obtains pardon; it is in dying that one is raised up to eternal life.
> - Saint Francis of Assisi, 1182 – 1226, Italian founder of the Franciscan Order of friars

There are certain laws that govern life, such as the law of cause and effect. In slang, it may be called, 'what goes around, comes around' or Karma. At school we learned about equal and opposite reactions. Another way to explain about Universal Truth is to say, 'what you give out, you get back'.

If you put out anger, you get anger back. If you put out happiness, you get happiness back. Put out love and that is what will be returned. Therefore, be generous with a loving attitude as this is the best way to receive abundance. This system of, 'what you put out is what you get back', or cause and affect, is not only taught in the Bible. It is taught by all major religions and is a cornerstone of their beliefs.

Generosity is not just giving money. It is giving of yourself, your compassion, time and love.

STOP
Who do you know that you can use as a 'generosity role model'?

....
....
....
....
....

> **STOP**
> **Are you generous of your self and not only with money?**

Are you generous? ....
....
....
....
....

The third pillar of Islam stipulates the practice of Alms giving (zakat). Generally speaking, it is the duty of a Believer to share his wealth with other members of the faith who are less well off or in need. The Koran teaches that the sharing must be given with a generous heart, and that like my friend Roy, giving quietly is valued more than doing so publicly.

There are many religious groups that swear to the benefits of tithing. They firmly believe that no matter how little they have, if they share they will receive a greater form of generosity some time in the future. They will never be left wanting.
If you are generous of nature and give of yourself, there is absolutely no doubt that you will receive love and support in a far greater proportion than you gave out. If you don't believe me, put it to the test.

Whatever you give away today or think or do, will return to you. It may not come immediately, nor from an obvious source, but the law applies unfailingly through some invisible force.

> **STOP**
> **Above I asked why you think there is a section on generosity in this book. Are you starting to get an understanding?**

Journal: ....
....
....
....
....

He that does good to another does good also to himself, not only in the consequence but in the very act. For the consciousness of well-doing is in itself ample reward.

– Seneca, C 4 BC – 65 AD, Roman Stoic playwright and author of many essays.

As we are part of mankind, let's emphasise the 'kind' part.

INTROSPECTION

Relax and slow down the mind for ten minutes. See yourself happily helping someone. This can be by giving of yourself and money. See yourself giving with a happy heart. When you are finished take note how you feel – good I bet.

Journal notes: ....
....
....
....
....

FINANCIAL AFFAIRS

Your relationship with money is a mirror of your relationship with yourself!

Your lack of money is an outward expression of your inner beliefs. Money, in itself, is meaningless. But as money has been elevated to being an indicator of success or failure, your inner self cleverly expresses its feelings through money. Money is, therefore, a reflection of your self-worth.

You may be able to earn big money, but can you hold onto it? You may have the discipline to retain money but can you earn it in large enough quantities for it to make a difference? Skill at handling money, more often than not, is overridden by your guiding belief.

Invariably a lack of money is an indication of a *'life that does not work'*.

There are those people who have lots of money but still have money issues, for example those who use it as a form of control. They may identify themselves with their money - it is who they are. Some cling to it as their security blanket.

By working on your money issues, you work on yourself. If you work on yourself you are likely to attract and hold on to more money. Find yourself and you are likely to find wealth.

Your financial worth is a result of those hidden and unseen thoughts. If your thoughts are self-limiting, it is likely that you will not have money in any reasonable quantity as money represents freedom, health (or improved health as a result of being able to afford a proper diet or to pay for medical bills, etc), reduced stress and improved self-esteem.

By being able to understand your unconscious feelings about money, you will learn about yourself.

Money matters are ever present in your life.

INTROSPECTION

Introspect on how your life is entwined with money. Look at your house and where you live and see how money influenced that decision. Where you go or don't go on holiday is a result of money you have or don't have. Quite often, the person you marry is influenced by his or her attitude to money as our partners can be a mirror reflection of us. The quality of your clothes, cars and surroundings are determined by money.

Notes on money……………………………………………………………………………………

………………………………………………………………………………………………………

………………………………………………………………………………………………………

………………………………………………………………………………………………………

Some limiting beliefs about money are:

- Money doesn't grow on trees.
- You have to work hard to earn money.
- People with money are evil.
- The rich get richer, the poor get poorer.

Now look at your attitude towards money. Based on what you determined above, do you think your beliefs are healthy? Does money empower or disempower you? Write down your thoughts in the journal. You may have to do this exercise several times to get the most from it.

Journal: ……………………………………………………………………………………………

………………………………………………………………………………………………………

………………………………………………………………………………………………………

………………………………………………………………………………………………………

………………………………………………………………………………………………………

A good relationship with money is likely to result in you accumulating more positive boxes (refer above). Conversely, more negative boxes are likely to result in a lack of money.

The promise of having or not having money
Not having money can set up fear in us, especially around bill time. Wanting money too badly can make us impatient. Impatience will block the receiving of money.

STOP
Are you a slave to your opinion about your financial status?

Journal: ....
....
....
....
....

Money Guilt

Many people feel guilty about wanting to be wealthy. Perhaps this is because their religion told them that vows of poverty are to be admired, or could it be that their philosophy books said that they should be aspiring towards altruism? Perhaps they come from a family where the belief is, *"money does not grow on trees"* or *"money corrupts."*

Well, I can tell you all this is baloney! Read what Fay Weldon (English novelist) says about money:

'Lack of money causes misery, anxiety, and early death: the cramping of personality, the limiting of human potential. Lack of money prevents us eating properly when we are children, ruins our health, rots our teeth. Lack of money makes our parents quarrel and take to drink. A lack of money stops us having the clothes we want, the friends we like, the parties we long for. Lack of money stops us having tuition, which would enable us to get an education - makes us end up street sweepers and not doctors. Lack of money induces women to have babies

because there is no money for travel or entertainment, or to leave the parental home any other way. A lack of money humiliates us all our lives.

'Lack of money makes us live with husbands or wives we no longer love. Lack of money makes us age earlier than we need. Lack of money makes our hands rough with toil and our brows crease with worry.

'Lack of money keeps us weeping by day and sleepless by night: the terror in our lives is the bill, which can't be paid. Our lives close in the knowledge of failure - we failed to make enough money. We never did what we wanted with our lives. How could we? We didn't have the money. We tell ourselves "money isn't important" but it is, it is. We couldn't afford this, we couldn't afford that, and our lives and our friendships and our marriages and our children were thereby curtailed, limited.'

Is that not brilliant writing and wisdom?

Look at what George Bernard Shaw (1856 - 1950, Critic and novelist) said about the subject: "Lack of money is the root of all evil."

STOP
Do you think living a life of poverty will bring you enlightenment?

Journal: ....
....
....
....
....

You want to help mankind? Well, the best way to help your fellow human beings is to become rich. By becoming wealthy you directly and indirectly give people employment. By becoming wealthy you create something out of nothing and in so doing, you contribute to the abundance of humanity. For instance, most of the charities of the world survive from the help of wealthy individuals and businesses. It is not the pennies put into collection boxes in shopping malls that keep these associations afloat. It is the philanthropy of the wealthy. Mother Teresa would probably not have achieved half as much without the financial generosity of wealthy individuals and companies.

The very best thing you can do for the world is to make the best of yourself and that also means becoming wealthy. From that platform you can help The Supreme Being and mankind in really meaningful ways. By remaining poor, you reduce your ability to help. If life is a struggle for survival, you are unable to give much of yourself or your time. Remember what was said earlier about my friend Roy? If he did not have spare cash, he would not have been able to help me or others as he has done. I in turn, have been able to help others and so it goes.

Remember the topic on *abundance*? - It is your birthright. By aligning yourself to Universal principles you can create plenty. When you create something out of nothing, you don't deprive anyone else, you're contributing. Every thought you have on financial matters is moulding your financial future.
Money is only energy (refer to the description of energy in Section One). Think of money as grains of sand on the longest beach you have ever seen. Know that there is plenty for everyone and it can never run out. As money is only energy, more can be created.

STOP
When you do the above exercise, how does it make you feel
– excited, guilty, happy, fearful?

....
....
....
....
....

INTROSPECTION

Go into introspection and visualise an amount greater than you are currently earning. When visualising, play an internal movie and…

- Change the value of your earnings.
- See the house you want.
- Appear in nice clothes, trendy and feeling successful. More importantly...
- Know that you are blessed with the ability to create your own abundance and that the only limitations are those that you impose.

Journal: ....
....
....
....
....

The feelings you have are good indicators of how you view money. It may be guilt or fear. Perhaps you have difficulty doing the exercise. If so, you need to re-examine your controlling beliefs.

STOP
Do you like money? Do you have a friendly relationship with it?

Journal: ....
....
....
....
....

If the answer to either of the above questions is no, then you will *not* manifest large sums of money.

Remember that changing from your current financial position to where you want to be will not happen overnight. You may have debts to clear or your income may be limited. By knowing and having faith that you are capable of creating what you want it will happen. You may need to start with small but positive steps.

Understand that your belief structure put you in your current financial position. It is up to you where you go on from here.

Two Aspects of Money
There are two aspects to money: the practical (correct management) and the spiritual. You require both to have money, for you to reap the full benefits of having money. The two aspects must be taken into account.

1) Let us talk about the spiritual first. Remember, money is only energy. We live in a world that is governed by energy. Everything in this universe is a vibration. It is all energy. We as humans are energy and vibration. We are made in the likeness of God who/which is also energy. The only differences are the rates of vibration. The more 'Divine-like' the faster the vibration is. Third dimensional man vibrates very slowly. Concrete, which is very dense, vibrates even more slowly. Aligning yourself to a spiritual life and having complete trust and faith will increase your vibration. Complete trust and faith means no negativity as negativity slows the vibration. Every time you doubt, you slow the vibration and move further away from your abundance.

2) Money Management is also where you let yourself down. For instance, money is more likely to slip through your fingers if you don't understand it. If you don't understand the principles of credit and interest or making money work for you, your money will not grow and you will never retain wealth. There are lots of people who are able to make money, but they cannot keep it. I know because I was one. My money skills were aligned to my lack of belief in myself. Consequently when I made some money, my script said, "You don't deserve this," so in a rash moment I would do "a deal" of some sort that would put me back two or three years.

In order to manage money, you have to understand yourself (yeah, there it is again) and seek out the patterns that you have created in your life. So often one hears someone say, "Gee, I thought I was just getting on top of things and wham, something stops working and it costs money to fix". You create your own *'broke syndrome'*. To break the cycle, you have to know what the cycle is, know where it comes from and then set about the mind changes to alter it.

The only purpose of money is to use it. Like everything else in life, it must flow, both in and out.

By setting financial goals, you have a method to measure your progress. If you do not have financial targets you have no standards to measure by. Set targets and monitor them on an ongoing basis.

Money is neither good nor bad. It is merely energy.
- Unknown

INTROSPECTION

Take time to learn how you feel about money.

- Do you have a healthy respect for it, and how it can serve you? Do you crave it too much?
- Do you find yourself challenging every purchase because you do not have enough?
- Do you always seem to be chasing it?
- Are you generous with it?

- Can you hang on to it?
- Are you wise with it?

Write down the answers to the above: ....
....
....
....
....
....

Money Mirror – *more ramblings of a writer*

Snug and warm in a cosy bar, with rain and a cold surf on the other side of the window, Crockie continued, '... and I really feel mankind is close to letting go of the curse of money ...'

'What would we want to do that for?' I interrupted him.

As I said this, he was about to sip his beer, but put it down and offered, 'Because money is the cause of so much that is wrong, and without money, humans would be better off. It causes major problems and taints the mind of many.' And then, as if to emphasise his point he took a long drink of his beer.

Trying to hide my mirth at the foam on his upper lip, which made him look like a middle-aged woman smeared with moustache remover, I said, 'Money is currency of another form, a reflection of our make-up at any given time. The manner in which we create or use money, and what we think about money, reveals what we think of ourselves; that is, provided we look.'

I continued my thoughts, 'A man-made illusion is using money as a measure of our own and each other's worth. If it were not money it would be cows, pieces of glass or pumpkins. There will always be a currency for barter and therefore a measure. Not being able to earn or hang on to that currency shouts loudly and clearly about who you are. So the state of a person's pumpkin will tell you a lot about the compost in the mind that grows it.'

I laughed at my joke, but he blurted, 'Crap, what about greed? Are you greedy?'

'Knowing how the universe works,' I said, 'I would find it difficult to be greedy.'

He looked in askance at me, so I continued, 'Because there is abundance for all, there is no need to be greedy. And if you put out greed, you'll get it back in some form or other. Look at currency this way. What better method is there to learn about yourself than through your relationship with money? After all, it is only energy.'

I took a sip of beer and said, 'Consider a person who is tight with money. What in their make-up instils a need to cling to it, like a toddler with a sweet, blurting out, "Mine"? Generous people are functional people while the greedy tend to lack something within. And those who broadcast their wealth are saying, 'Please look at me, here I am.'

On a roll, I continued, 'What about those who believe they are not valuable enough and give themselves nought?'

'Yeah, that happens,' he agreed.

The last thing that I wanted to tell him was, 'Not having any money in the bank right now may not point to a problem as that person may be on a positive path and so the bucks will in time, catch up with their attitude.'

Pointing to my empty glass, I said, 'And by the way, your round.'

GOAL SETTING = A road map and compass to a definite destination

Just as there are laws relating to physics, there are laws for goal setting.   *- Unknown*

By setting goals, you are forced to have total clarity of thought. If the mind is not clear on what you want, how can it work in your favour?

If you don't plan something today, you will have less of something tomorrow. If you don't know what you want, how will you know when you achieve it?

When the mind has a known target, it can FOCUS and DIRECT and RE-FOCUS and RE-DIRECT until it reaches the intended goal. If a person does not have a defined target his/her effectiveness is diminished.

Have you ever tried to put together a jigsaw puzzle without having seen the picture of what it represents? That's what happens when you try and put your life together without planning the outcome.

Life's goals must be so clear that any decisions, (that affect your future) can be evaluated against them.

Day by day nothing seems to change, but pretty soon everything's different.   *- Calvin Hobbs*

STOP
Do you know what the price is?
Are you willing to pay it?

....
....
....
....

After setting goals, you must live the desired results, even if they have not been achieved. Remember I said earlier on that when we aspire to become something or accomplish some task, we have to take on that persona. For instance, I have a friend who wants to become an author. To meet this end, she writes short stories and works on her technical skills. Yet, when speaking to her she talks about the time when she will be a writer. In her mind she would not dare tell people that she is a writer, not until she has been published. This is wrong. You become a writer the minute that you put your mind to it. It does not matter what other people think or your level of skill at that point in time. There is a mental barrier that will hold you back and sap your ability. If you play the part, it is more likely that you will become the part. Then guess what happened to her? A magazine published an article of hers but she still didn't call herself a writer, either aloud to others or to herself, just in case it was a fluke. Her talent is slowly emerging but if only she looked at it from a different perspective she would have been published much earlier. Remember what I said about being it, to become it. She is not being it, so it is unlikely that she will become it.

When you set goals, understand that there is a price. The price could be:

- A million hours on the golf course
- Thousands of lengths of the pool
- Studying to the small hours of the morning
- Going that extra mile so you can advance
- Working instead of having fun
- Working at a place you don't like in order to learn new skills

> **STOP**
> Do you have a dream that you aspire to, but still do not regard yourself as living that dream now?
> For instance, a dream to become an actor while not calling yourself an actor, or to paint while not considering yourself an artist?

What are those dreams? ....
....
....
....
....

You put in effort in the short term, so you can have it in the long term.

STOP
Do you know what the price is and are you willing to pay it?

Journal: ....
....
....
....
....

By definition, to be successful you must have goals as goals are measurable and a yardstick. No goals = no success. *If you have no goals, how do you know if you are on target?*

If you don't know where you are going, then it doesn't matter how long it takes to get there.

Until one is committed, there is hesitance, the chance to withdraw, ineffectiveness. Concerning all acts of initiative (and creation) there is one elementary truth, the ignorance of which kills countless ideas and splendid plans. The moment one commits oneself, Providence moves too. All sorts of things occur to help one that would never otherwise have happened. A whole stream of events issues from the decision, raising in one's favour all manner of unforeseen incidents, meetings and material assistance, which one could never have dreamed would have come their way.
                                              - Goethe

Whatever you can do, or dream you can begin it. Boldness has genius, power and magic in it. Begin it now.
                    -Johann Wolfgang von Goethe, 1749 – 1832
                                     (German poet, novelist)

Can you honestly say that you are committed to your goals?

....
....
....
....

Your Personal Life Plan

I always wanted to be somebody, but I should have been more specific.   - Jane Wagner (and Lily Tomlin)

JOURNAL WRITING AND INTROSPECTION (Set aside at least an hour.

Now is your chance to be more specific and to determine who you want to be in the future. In the journal part, you will see in the heading: <u>Who Do I Want To Become?</u> Spend at least half an hour, writing down your thoughts as you create your vision for the new you. Write them down as if you were already that person - I am a famous author.

You determine who that person is going to be. Re-read this section on goal setting and then lower your mind to the alpha state as you have been taught. Allocate a good half an hour as you prepare yourself for more clarity by going into an introspection.

When there, consider who you would like to be. Take your time to understand what goals would be worthy of your attention. There should be **short**, **intermediate** and **long-term** goals. Set different goals for your personal life and work.

You may need a few separate introspections to focus on different goals. In fact it is a good idea to do these on an ongoing basis and each time record the requirements in your journal.

When you have decided on each goal, set a time to do another introspection. In this new introspection, see yourself as already having achieved it, as per the first short term aspiration. Use all your visualisation techniques. The more often you do this visualisation, the sooner you will align yourself with who you want to be. Reinforce your goals often by re-reading your journal.

Another beneficial introspection is one where you see yourself having achieved a goal, but then backtracking to see what steps were needed to get there.

Don't be afraid to amend your goals from time to time.

A note on visualisation: The universe does not work on your time frame so don't become impatient if nothing seems to happen initially. If you are diligent and consistent, you will see results. These can manifest immediately or could take as long as three months for an improvement. Remember you must remain positive!

Some people cannot see pictures in their mind. This is OK and if you are one of these people, I suggest that you cut pictures out of magazines and papers and make a 'vision board'. You then spend focus time on the board.

Do you know who you want to become? ……………………………………………………

………………………………………………………………………………………………………

………………………………………………………………………………………………………

………………………………………………………………………………………………………

………………………………………………………………………………………………………

………………………………………………………………………………………………………

………………………………………………………………………………………………………

………………………………………………………………………………………………………

………………………………………………………………………………………………………

Now sign what you have just written……………………………………………………………

HAPPINESS

"Happiness is the meaning and purpose of life, the whole aim and end of human existence", declared Aristotle.

Joy or happiness?

I would like to make a distinction between being happy and being joyous. Being happy can result from an external event and is therefore out of your control and short-lived. Joy is a deep emotion of pleasure, gladness.

So although I talk about happiness, I really mean joy.

Your Choice

Being either happy or unhappy is a choice. Choose to be happy today or choose to be sad today, it is up to you.

Most folks are about as happy as they make up their minds to be. — Abraham Lincoln

Over drinks one night, a friend told me that she is as about as happy as she can be. Knowing her as I do, this is not very happy. She equates **relative** peace with happiness. What she meant by relative peace, is where things don't go badly.

Pondering what she said, I later emailed her the following: *I am intrigued with your concept that peace is also happiness. I think that peace does not necessarily equate to happiness, it can be an acceptance of the status quo, but not necessarily joy. However, you are partly right in thinking that peace is what is required, because certainly there can be no happiness without peace, but peace does not ensure happiness.*

Although happiness is within us, we have to bring it to the fore. We do this from a positive and willing mind-set and a firm belief that life is good. We also do it for the knowledge that in action there is hope.

How do you know if you are unhappy or sad? You introspect. Take the time to regularly stop and monitor just how you feel. <u>How do you feel right now?</u> Look within. After a while you will get the essence of whether you are happy or miserable. If you are the latter then invoke the power of choice. Change your thoughts that contribute to your dissatisfaction.

STOP
Sit and calm your mind for a ten minute period
(have a watch next to you). Just think happy thoughts.
You are likely to feel a warm spot in your tummy or heart.
Record your findings.
You'll be amazed at how good this can make you feel.

Journal: ....
....
....
....
....

When you are happy you will have more friends (who would gravitate to a ball of misery?), your levels of stress will be lower - therefore, you will be healthier. I am sure you have heard the saying, *'Laughter is the best medicine'.*

STOP
Are you generally a happy person? If not, why not?

Journal: ....

....

....

....

....

....

Happiness Comes From Within

The happiness that I refer to is not the short-lived mirth that you get from a joke. It is a deep sense of contentment that comes from within. True happiness comes from the simple things in life.

As we are the artists of our own thoughts, it is reasonable to argue that we create the scenes that hang on the walls of our minds. If you cannot find contentment inside, it is useless looking outside.

Happiness is now, not tomorrow or the day after.

The best preparation for a better life next year, is to be happy now.

Dale Carnegie (author of *How to Win Friends and Influence People*, 1888 – 1955) said "One of the most tragic things I know about human nature is that all of us tend to put off living. We are all dreaming of some magical rose garden over the horizon – instead of enjoying the roses that are blooming outside our window today".

Being happy is the best insurance against old age, the best medicine for health and the surest way to have friends.

- Unknown

To Change

How do you change from being a sad person to a happy one? The first thing is to acknowledge that you are predominantly unhappy and from that base set about to positively improve your mental outlook. You cannot chase happiness, you must BE happiness. You do not have to search far and wide for it, it's there already. You cannot buy happiness as it is within you, a state of mind. Are you happy now? If not, choose to move towards happiness. If you don't choose to be happy, fine, stay sad, stay angry, remain unforgiving, be a complainer and continue a life that does not work!

- As happiness comes from within, you must make a habit of it. Unhappiness is also a habit.
- As happiness comes from within, it is not dependent on where you live or who your partner is or isn't.
- True happiness is not achieved by wealth. Wealth may make life easier but wealth on its own will not create true and lasting joy.

Man is the only creature on earth that can be perpetually miserable. Dogs, cats, birds and all the other animals seem happy. Dogs are probably the best at showing their happiness by wagging their tails. You can see the happiness in their eyes. Unlike humans, dogs are not afraid to express their happiness.

Laughter

Mel Brooks says - "Humour is just another defence against the universe."

Did you know that you can't laugh and be angry at the same time?

Research at Clark University USA indicated that smiling creates mood changes for the better. Try belly laughing - it really helps. Always try to be happy and feel like laughing all the times.

Smile at people then watch the smiles return tenfold. Apparently it takes 65 muscles to frown and only 25 to smile.

The best way to measure your day's success is by the number of smiles or laughs you have had.

> **STOP**
> **Think back on your day so far and see how many times you laughed. You would do well to laugh at least once per hour.**

....
....
....

There's no point in being grown up if you can't be childish sometimes.
— Doctor Who, TV show

I am a kind of paranoiac in reverse. I suspect people of plotting to make me happy.
— J.D. Salinger

Happiness and Material Possessions

Having a fortune will not make you happy. Being an intellectual will not make you happy. Being healthy will not make you happy. Only *you* will make *you* happy.

Don't set conditions for being happy, e.g. 'I'll be happy when I have this or that'.

It is only possible to live happily ever after on a day-to-day basis.
— Margaret Bonnano

> **STOP**
> **Do you mourn the things that you do not have? Or anguish over what you are not?**

Journal: ....
....
....

....
....

Be grateful for what you do have. Happiness is not in having or achieving, happiness just is.

The grass may appear to be greener on the other side but unless you are internally happy you will not be any happier for going there.

If you want to encourage happiness, don't criticise others as this just creates stress. Being aggressive is a contradiction to happiness.

Happiness and Purpose

Purpose in life helps creates joy. No purpose in life leads to a lack of joy. When you have a fulfilling life you are more likely to have a happy one or when you are happy you are more likely to feel fulfilled. To achieve your purpose, you need optimism. **Do you know any happy pessimists?**

STOP
Do you know your purpose? You should, it is to be happy.

Journal: ....
....
....
....
....

Happiness and Work

Few people realise how important their work is in their quest to achieve happiness. As our job constitutes such a large part of our lives, it is imperative to be content at work.

INTROSPECTION

If you are unhappy with your job, why. Is it the actual work or the company, or is it your mind that makes you unhappy? Whatever, rectify it. You are powerful beyond belief and are able to change your attitude. Write down your findings in your journal.
Journal: ....

....
....
....
....

One of my favourite inspirers, Ralph Waldo Emerson, declared: "Happiness is perfume you cannot pour on others without getting a few drops on yourself."

Laughter is the sunshine of the soul.   *– Dr Wayne Dyer*

Joy comes from a contented mindset

HEALTH

It is well known that most disease is caused by the mind.

Caroline Myss (spiritual teacher, intuitive and author), says, "Our biography is our biology."

A lot of psychologists will tell you that people don't really want to be cured. What they want is relief. Cure is painful! In fact they want instant TV dinner type of relief. Healing is taking responsibility for your thoughts and understanding yourself. Healing can take ages or it can take minutes. It depends on your mind-set. If there have been years of degeneration then healing is unlikely to be quick. But it may only take minutes to commence the reversal of degeneration. It is up to you.
Over the years much has been said about the necessity of good diet and exercise for maximum health. Of course this is correct. But not much has been said about how good diet and exercise can be negated if our minds or attitudes to life are wrong. We, or rather our minds, influence the health of our bodies. If our thought processes are cock-eyed we are likely to have some form of physical discomfort no matter how many nuts we consume.

If as stated above under HAPPINESS IN LIFE, you are a habitually stressed-out morose person then your health will be affected. Conversely, by being happy you will reduce your medical bills. If you let stressful situations direct your thought processes, you will 'internalise' right down to the cellular level and once this occurs, you will be well on your way to illness. Over time and with a constant bombardment of negativity, imperfect health can develop into something sinister like cancer or high blood pressure. Therefore, your thoughts create health or dis-ease in the body.

As with a lot of other issues in this book, your health comes down to choice. Do you choose the right thoughts, to be peaceful and content or do you choose the wrong thoughts and to be unhealthy?

LOVE

Most authors avoid writing about love or only skirt around the topic. They may be wiser than me. Nevertheless I am going to attempt to put love into perspective.

The reason why a discussion on love is necessary is because without love, everything else is irrelevant. It is imperative that you understand how love forms the basis of everything you are.

Firstly, we will look at what love is, and see how ambiguous love is to describe. Then we will look at romantic love and finally spiritual love.

We said earlier that we do not have the ability to understand what The Supreme Being is, as it is just too vast for our mind to grasp. The same applies to Love. Love is an intangible and as such is difficult to describe.

STOP
Do you think that the difficulty in describing God and Love
is because God and Love are one and the same thing?

Journal: ....
....
....
....
....

It was Confucius who said that "We do not know what we do not know."

Even though it seems that we do not know both God and Love, it doesn't mean that they aren't real.

Love

Love describes an attitude or a state of mind. Love is also a verb as in 'I love you'. Love is also a noun (his love of music)

STOP
Having read these definitions, are you any closer to understanding what love is?

Journal: ....
....
....
....
....

Love is patient and kind, it is not jealous or conceited or proud. Love is not ill-mannered or selfish or irritable: love does not keep a record of wrongs: Love never gives up faith. Hope and patience never fail. Love is eternal. Meanwhile these three remain: faith, hope and love: and the greatest of these is love.

Corinthians 13

Love is a state of mind, a way of being, a form of happiness and an enjoyable emotion. You can't feel love and not be happy at the same time.

Love and the Great Religious Teachings

All the great religions have love as their core belief. The KJV01 Bible talks of love no less than **304 times**. Here is an example - "**God is love and he who abides in love abides in God and God abides in him**."

The Buddha espoused love as one of the main tenets for a worthwhile life: "And he that loveth not, knoweth not God. For God is love."

Love, Faith and Trust

A friend recently said that she associates love with pain. How sad. Love does not have to be like this. It depends on you.
If you are like the friend who associates love with pain, the best way to learn what love really represents to you, is to give out love at each and every opportunity.

Remember, love can be expressed as an action - therefore be of a loving mind for those who cross your path. It will not be long before love starts to return to you. From there it will grow.

Many associate 'romantic love' with pain because of its transient nature. It cannot be healed unless we understand our programming and perceptions about love. We are taught that 'love' will make us happy. That is all we are told about love. We do not realise that 'romantic love' is an illusion – that 'romantic love' (or that temporary happy feeling that comes with it), may or may not grow into a deep and lasting love that would surpass and exist after the 'romantic feeling' is gone.

A tremendous musician, John Lennon's greatest contribution to mankind was expressing the words, **"All you need is love"**. The awareness that he created for millions of people around the world is nothing short of amazing. Over forty years later Lennon is still renowned for preaching love and respect for each other.

Are you Open to Love? Can you receive love?

For example, a friend offers you a gift but you do not accept it because you feel guilty. Although you don't admit your guilt, you tell your friend that you could not possibly accept it. Your lack of self-worth says, 'I am not good enough to be given anything'. This is the same as feeling you are not worthy of being loved.

What is Love to Me?

I cannot tritely say that **love is all there is.** I could say that we do not possess enough knowledge or have the communication skills to correctly describe love - and leave it at that. I offer the following which helps me to understand what love is:

Snapshot

When I was about four and I was put into the orphanage, there was no love there. It was emotionally cold and barren. I remember the day my brother John and I were 'released' and returned to my father and his new wife. She became 'my mother'. It was a few days after Christmas. But, what was Christmas? I didn't know. I learned quickly enough when we arrived at the house they had bought. The house became a home - 'my home'. It was a strange house because inside there was a tree growing in the lounge! Under the tree were brightly-wrapped parcels. All these years later I still remember what my present was - it was a blue and white speedboat. Later that day we went to the beach for my first swim. The boat came with me. That day is etched into my mind. The sky was deep blue and the sun radiated love and warmth, but best of all I was with my family. For the first time in my young life, I felt wanted, secure and loved. That day was love!

As a kid growing up and having animals, I felt love. They taught me about total uncompromising and unconditional love. This I learned from our various dogs. I was influenced by their bright-eyed, 'waggy tail love' and learnt to give them the love that was innately a part of me (and that which is innately a part of you) and this allowed me to receive the love they gave me.

My Brother John

Recently my brother John visited from Australia, where we toured the country together. Of course we reminisced about all the fun that we had as kids. But when talking about some of the not-so-nice times, he told me that he does not remember the orphanage or the farm - his mind has blocked these things! He went on to tell me that his first memories are of that very same day I just described. As far as his memory is concerned, the first day of his life was when he was six years old.
I was flabbergasted, because I had written about that day in my writings many years earlier. I never knew that it was John's first memory. How sad that his life was so traumatised that he has no earlier memories. Conversely how wonderful that the day I describe as being one of love is the same day that is his first memory.

There has been an on-going research programme into prisoners and love in some of the prisons of the Western Cape of South Africa, where prisoners are encouraged to take on a pet. Invariably by owning a cat, a dog or a bird (or any other animal), it doesn't take long before the prisoners love these pets. Apparently for some, their view of life has changed and levels of aggression reduced. This is understandable as to look after a pet usually en(tails) giving of yourself (which is love) and for the first time in their lives, they gave something without expecting something back.

A thought on the above. There are some people who love their animals, but they don't trust themselves or others enough to allow love into their life from that of a potential partner. This is sad, as their fear limits or restricts the love that they could give, but more importantly, they reduce the love that they could receive.
I have said in this book that *there are no bad people, only people who do bad things* (their behaviour is not who they are). The prisoners' pets programme clearly brings out the good in people who are considered bad. *As I grew up, I got into relationships where I gave love and felt what love was like from another person other than a relative. It may have been puppy love, but it was great. Then I got married and found deeper levels of love that I had no idea existed. My children then arrived and added another dimension to love.*

Currently I am in a relationship where I have never felt so cherished or loved. I in return have such deep reserves of love that what I can give or do for my partner seems limitless. Clearly the love that we can both give and receive is a result of the belief and confidence that we have in ourselves. The levels of trust that we have are indicative of the trust that we have in a benevolent God. Our relationship works because we do not bring fear to it. Throughout this book, I have stressed how much work I have done on myself. My girlfriend is also the end product of the work that she has done on herself. The result is that we come together without the need for the other. We join in union without fear. And lastly, we both bring unconditional love to the table.

Continuing with how I see love: Growing older, I learnt that there was yet another type of love to be had or given. And that is Universal love. This may be the best love of all as it comes from deep within and requires no partner, mother or father. All it requires is a willingness to see good in all people and situations and to actively express it. What we get in return is truly amazing.

INTROSPECTION

In today's introspection, look at the times you have known love and re-live the joy of those times. Record them in your journal.

Journal: ....

....

....

STOP
Can you add any insights about what Love is to you?
Once you record them you will be able to start living them
in a better way than perhaps you do now.

....

....

....

Love is not external to us. It is inside us when we are born. We don't have to go looking for love as we already have it. It is like the air that we breathe, we cannot see it but it is there for us to use. To release love all we need is an awareness and a willingness. When we call for it, it will erupt.

Other Thoughts on Love

There is an abundance of love; grab as much as you want. However, there is a rule; *you can only receive love when you give out love.* The more you give out the more you receive.

If you cannot love yourself, you can't love anyone else.

To love your fellow man means letting go of judgement.

Universal Love

> **STOP**
> **What do you think John Lennon really meant when he said, "All you need is Love"? What does Christianity and all the other religions mean when they talk about love, or Universal love?**

Journal: ....
....
....
....
....

Who inspires you because they live and demonstrate love most of the time?
....
....
....
....

Universal love is our ability to love all people, not just the chosen few who are in our immediate orbit. The feeling of love we have for our wives, husbands or children is extended from our close family to beyond the walls of our homes to the most distant village, town or country. We feel that same love for the dwellers of those near and far places.

Universal love is taking that same love and extending it to things as well as people, to animals and happenings.

When we love our wives or girlfriends, we *love* the feeling of love, yet we only seem capable of loving a handful of people at any one time. Imagine having that same wonderful feeling of love expanded a 1000 or 10,000 times? This is what I believe that the teachings of Christianity and other major religions refer to when they talk about the 'bliss' of love.

You may ask me, "Have you reached that point of Universal Love?" To be honest, no I haven't, but I am striving towards it. I started with the handful of people around me and then extended it to those I come into contact with on a regular basis. I will keep extending it until I leave this planet - it is ongoing.

STOP
Based on what you just read, what do you think is the foundation you need?

Journal notes: ....
....
....
....
....

By now, you should know the answer - It is being clear of issues. You can't love all that there is if you are dysfunctional, unhappy, angry, fearful, unforgiving or have a life that doesn't work. There has to be contentment and trust.

Compassion and generosity are both expressions of love

Love and Meditation

I have absolutely no doubt that the more one meditates, the closer one moves to the ideal of love. I have noticed this in myself and also others who meditate on a regular basis.

Love is where personality and God merge

Spiritual love can be seen from the following

- Kindness
- Caring, not just for people close to you, but caring for people you don't know, for animals and for the planet.
- Compassion
- Joy
- An appreciation of everything around you

- It's easy to forgive
- A generous giving of yourself
- There is no judgement of others
- Acts of service
- You are beyond ego

Pierre Teilhard de Chardin taught: "love is the affinity which links and draws the elements of the world together".

Love is the driving force for the highest values of human life; to the power of truth, knowledge, beauty, freedom, goodness and happiness.
- Pitirim Soroken

Love (Relationships)

Whoa! How can I, with all the mistakes that I have made, try to advise you on love, romance or relationships? Perhaps the word 'mistakes' is the operative word - I should be good at this topic as I have made many!

I have included a section on romantic love because most of us, at some time during our lives, have had at least one partner. The partner may change from time to time, but that doesn't matter as we will be in a better position to manage our relationships when we understand ourselves. By knowing ourselves as we should, it will help in understanding the strengths and weaknesses of our partner. For instance, what mode of behaviour would a person bring to the partnership if they were afraid of abandonment?

This was my fear as a result of my mother's departure. It could be that your partner is so fear based that s/he will not commit to you.

You will see that by contemplating your issues in relationship you will gain insight and guidance.

STOP
Before we continue, look at the relationships in your life (past and present). Your partners have been your teachers as you have been theirs. Record what they have taught you about yourself and about your fears.

Journal: ....
....
....
....
....
....
....

Snapshot

*Throughout my life, I felt that my adverse early start had made me stronger and tougher and that I could control and work through any situation. In actual fact, all I did was to hide the fear with a sort of bravado. I put it all in a concrete bunker thinking I had disposed of it. But like nuclear waste, the threat was ever present and one day I had to face up to the issues **that actually controlled me**. I had always worked on my self intellectually (masculine) and not emotionally (feminine) and so never understood rejection. Intellectually I thought that by accepting the past that I would be free of issues. The reality was that on an emotional level, deep down I was wounded. The wounds set up a script, one that said **I was not good enough**. My intellect attempted to counteract this with control - a control my poor partners had to endure. Some who had been close to me said that **I never gave all of my self, something was hidden or lacking**. Clearly, I did not risk total exposure.*

Yet, for some of my past relationships, the same pattern emerged, and so in one way or another, the relationships ended and I was left compromised and hurt.

*Adding to the turmoil was the fact that I did not embrace the feminine side of myself, that is, the gentle and soft and passive part of me. This was partially due to my Australian background; at the time it was considered weak to be anything other than in control and the **'man of the house'**, with a capital M. But somewhere inside of me, I knew this to be folly and so had a pushme-pullme tug-of-war. I am not gay and never had any tendencies to be so, yet my love affairs would have been smoother if I let that more gentle part of my character out. I am now able to do so.*

But in the past my conditioning ruled me and therefore I controlled. Moreover, as an Aries star sign, coming from the planet 'God of War', the need for the masculine side was accentuated.

Everything in life has an opposite and by suppressing my feminine side and accentuating the masculine, chaos reined. I had to learn that it was OK to not be in control and I learned to back off. In fact, it is my feminine self that is now writing this. The same process occurred, not only in my love relationships, but also in business relationships.

All those past love affairs were fraught with power struggles. I was terrified that my partner would leave me, just as my mother did when I was two. She was my support structure that fed, bathed and loved me. When she withdrew, I lost faith in women.

As an adult, ruled by a two year old mind set, **I had to protect myself from this recurring** *and so I rigidly controlled my home life by putting in place a defence system. The two-year old in me decided that never again would anyone abandon me. Remember on some level, all my partners were my mother. Most of my love affairs ended with me leaving them, invariably in panic. I had to show them that I was in control and was not dependent on them. Of course I was dependent and very much out of control. All of this was on a subconscious level, a level that was constantly churning and bubbling. On a conscious level, I was able to justify my behaviour and rationalised it as, 'she was such a negative person that I couldn't let myself be dragged into her negativity'. Not, that I was scared, because she didn't make a commitment, as I wanted it to be. Or, '***she is so full of fear***, when in actual fact, it was me who was the one in fear'. None of my partners were stupid and could see that my imposed control stated, '***I don't trust you***', and so they erected their own defences, which would be the beginning of the end. I would tell them that I loved them and in fact did, but my actions suggested fear.*

Fortunately, I now relax and back off, to dismantle the fence and let my feminine side smile. I understood my fears and was able to work through them and as I did I was also able to work through the emotions. I will continue to do this, knowing that it is an ongoing process, my life's work.

STOP
Do you relate to any of the above?

Journal notes: ....
....
....
....
....

Some of the Things that I do Know About Love

- If you love someone, do not hold back, be committed and love with all your being. If you hold back because of fear or a lack of trust, I guarantee the relationship will end or be dysfunctional.
- About romantic love: do not tell someone you love them if you don't, but do tell those that you love and tell them every day.
- Be careful to monitor the negativities of your partner. These could be fears or insecurities that are likely to affect you in a negative way. Ensure that your ego or small self does not feel compromised. These would be mirrors of you.
- When starting a relationship have no expectations. That way you are less likely to get hurt. Be open to the growth when it arrives.

- You hear people say, "You complete me." Does this mean that before they met 'the one', they were in bits? Be sure you feel complete within yourself, are self-reliant and are not waiting to be rescued.
- You will not (or should not try to) change your partner. If communication does not resolve your issues then do what is best for both of you - part company!
- Before you get involved and make a commitment to someone, don't let lust, desperation, immaturity, ignorance, pressure from others or low self-esteem blind you.
- We need to be loved for who we are, not for what we do. Conversely, love your loved one for who she/he is, not for what you want them to be.
- It is possible to love someone who is not good for you. No matter how hard you try, you may not overcome obstacles to find common ground. Yes, it can happen, I know, I have been there! Fortunately I could see and accept this and get out.
- The older we get the more baggage we are likely to accumulate. This baggage equates to fear, which can be harder to trust a new partner. So when entering a new relationship, you have to be brave and have the strength of character to not let your demons rule, or get scared as a result of your partners demons that will surely emerge.
- Love must be learnt, either through interaction with our family when in infancy, or as a result of searching for how to love. But learnt it must be.
- Leo Buscaglia in his book, *Born for Love* wrote: "The most fulfilling goal in life is to love and to be loved. Money, fame, and possessions are generally more desired, because we wrongly assume that if we succeed in these ways, love will flow from them. Nothing can be further from the truth!"
- No matter our age, we need love and we search for it our entire lives.

Do not be in a relationship because you do not want to be alone.

Humans were born to be part of a group, yet at the same time, we are solitary by nature. We forget this and panic if we do not surround ourselves with things or people to clutter up our time.

When in a relationship, we are ultimately still alone. It is not advisable to enter into a relationship merely to fill up empty spaces in your life. Even within relationships, it is recommended that you spend time on your own. This will help you to refresh and balance your perspective. By doing so, you will energise your love for that special person.

Relationships are an express route to finding out about yourself. Whatever your major fears or modes of behaviour, these will be presented to you in all their detail.

Recently I had lunch with a girl who has a fear about men's lack of integrity. She went on to tell me that she had had numerous boyfriends who in one form or another betrayed her. Several had been unfaithful and several had hurt her by trampling the trust that she extended. I pointed out the connection between her fear and the actual happenings and said that until she relaxes her fear, it will continue to recur.

Lessons through relationships

Two paragraphs above I said; Relationships are an express route to finding out about your self. Adding to this, failed relationships also teach you about yourself as will your time in-between relationships. For instance, many people find being on their own a challenge as they have to face up to their feelings of inadequacy. They have a need to fill the gap by entering a relationship. If they do, it may seem that they are overcoming their feelings of inadequacy, when they are merely masking them. If your relationships continue to have conflict, the reason could be that you use relationships to validate yourself.

Earlier on in this work I said that dependency is a limitation and clearly being in a relationship for the wrong reasons means you are dependent.

INTROSPECTION

Run a movie in your head on each of your past relationships. Record the main theme that came up with each. Is there a pattern? What have you learned that can help you in the future? What do these trends tell you about yourself and your needs?

Journal notes: ....
....
....
....
....
....

Conditional, Unconditional or Possessive Love

> **STOP**
> **How do you love, is it unconditional,**
> **conditional or possessive?**

Journal: ....
....
....
....

....
....

What do we mean by unconditional love? Well, when you think about the person whom you love, do you have a warm feeling or do you intellectualise it in your head? Stuff like, *he is always doing that* or feelings of anger or resentment? The warm feeling is unconditional, the other is your enemy.

The way I understand unconditional love is that your love for a person is not conditional upon their behaviour or what you can get out of them, or what they give to you. Unconditional love separates the essence of a person from outer characteristics. It is constant and dependable and no change in exterior circumstances can alter it, e.g. the love of a parent for their child.

STOP
Is your love possessive? Do you need to cling to your loved one, always needing to be with them and not letting them out of your sight? Do you have a cold feeling in your stomach if you see them talking to someone of the opposite sex? If so, this is possessive. Possessiveness is a direct result of a lack of trust. This type of love is more often than not in the relationships of younger people, people who are still to find themselves.

Journal: ....
....
....
....

Both possessive and conditional love comes from your head, so get out of there, it's a bad neighbourhood to be in.

It is better to focus on love. If there is no love, or the partner is really difficult, then leave the relationship. Awareness and understanding are paramount in having great relationships.

STOP
I said above that relationships are an express way of learning about yourself. If you realise that you are possessive in your relationships, what does this tell you about yourself?

Journal notes: ....
....
....
....
....

As a child, did you feel rejected? If so, let go of the need for dependence on another. Don't be clingy.

Do not look at changing people, look at changing the way you think about them!
Jealousy

Do you get jealous about your partners? If so, it is not the partner that is the problem, it is you. What is within you that says, *because I am not good enough, she will leave?*

STOP
Have you been jealous in your past relationships?
Take time to really look at this. Look at the feelings you had, the pain, and try and work out why. Record this in your journal.

Journal: ....
....
....
....
....

The easiest kind of relationship for me is with ten thousand people. The hardest is with one. — Joan Baez, singer

Love works miracles every day: such as weakening the strong, and strengthening the weak; making fools of the wise, and wise men of fools; favouring the passions, destroying reason, and, in a word turning everything topsy. — Unknown

And lastly Samuel Butler: "It is better to have loved and lost than never to have loved at all."

MORAL CODE/ETHICS
A Moral Code = Smooth sailing

When you die, you will be remembered for the essence of who you were and not necessarily for your successes.

A moral code reflects your respect for humanity, your business associates and your family. In addition, a well-structured moral code mirrors your opinion of yourself.

Well-developed ethics are a guiding light. It takes the uncertainty out of questionable decision-making and negates the likelihood of guilt. You are also likely to attract people into your life with a similar code of ethics as your own, so it makes sense to develop a meaningful code.

This is a big subject, one that requires total honesty and dedication, a subject that needs heart-rending assessment and continued application.

The Concise Oxford Dictionary on Morals defines morality/morals as: A concern with character or disposition, with the distinction between right and wrong.

If we are to be Divine in nature there can be no grey areas. In order to eliminate the grey areas, we have to understand what the white and the black areas are. Those who have a deep sense of what is right and what is wrong are a lantern to guide others by.

Moral Code and Conforming

Conforming = Limitation

When you define your moral code, look very closely at issues of conformity. Don't decide what is white or black because culture suggests so. Know your own mind by setting your own standards.

We conform to society's dress codes and behavioural codes i.e. *the latest in-thing!* A friend of mine wears the most outlandish clothes, some of which only just cover her (even in winter). She wears these as an expression of who she is. The best part is that she doesn't care if people deride her. She remains totally unconcerned. Her freedom in this area of her life is refreshing. By not conforming, her personality shines through.

Are you a conformist? ....

When people are free to do as they please, they usually imitate each other.
— Eric Hoffer

When all think alike, no one is thinking very much.
— Unknown

Whoso would be a man must be a non-conformist.
— Ralph Waldo Emerson in his essay *Self-Reliance*.

STOP
Do you forfeit much of your life to be like other people?
Is it worth it? Do you conform so that you can be liked?

Answers: ………………………………………………………………………
……………………………………………………………………………………
……………………………………………………………………………………
……………………………………………………………………………………
……………………………………………………………………………………

Consistency

I knew a girl who always had to win. She was a nice girl and basically honest, except when it came to arguments. She had to win! She would say things that were untrue, and things that were meant to hurt. Afterwards she would conveniently forget what she had said. She had an intermittent moral code. She turned the standards on and off when it suited her.

This girl could have been a friend of Groucho Marx, who said, "Those are my principles. If you don't like them I have others!"

Have you ever known someone who was in a marriage and was unfaithful to their partner? They probably justified it by saying, 'It's OK because we don't get on well." or 'He is nasty' or 'She drinks too much'. If that were the case and the relationship wasn't working, that person could have chosen to get out, instead of using somebody else's bad behaviour to justify their lack of ethics. Don't remain in situations that could compromise your standards.

In sports as in other parts of your life, do you have standards that you will not breach? If you were a runner or cyclist and you were in a race, would you cut a corner illegally if you thought no one could see you? Or if you were playing cards, would you sneak a look at the other person's hand? Would you move your ball to a better lie whilst playing golf if you thought no one could see? By doing these things, you would only be cheating yourself.

STOP
What is it in you that needs a winner's
pat on the back, irrespective of the cost?

Journal notes: ....
....
....
....
....
....

INTROSPECTION

Prepare yourself and introspect on your moral code. Which of your ethics would you never compromise and which of them are merely restrictions placed on you by society or your religious beliefs? Write down the answers. Expand on this as time goes on.

Journal: ....
....
....
....
....
....
....

Self Determination

We have to set our own moral codes, as external regulation holds no value for us. Lack of integrity can be broken down into the categories of falsehood, deceit, hypocrisy and illegal gain. Some failings are quite obvious, such as telling a lie or stealing. Other transgressions may be subtle and we may not even be aware of the indiscretion, for example, seducing a girl because she was interested in you, even though you had no real interest in her.

Once we understand ourselves better and increase our awareness, we are more able to own our truth and take responsibility for our actions, e.g. an employee hides the fact that a certain job hasn't been done for fear of losing his job. People lie to their family and friends to cover up failure or disgrace. In many cases people lie to retain an image they wish to project.

Don't ever sacrifice your morals for financial or personal gain, especially in a business situation. There is a difference between being astute and being unethical. You do not have to resort to devious tactics. Rather be smart and creative.

Contravention of your moral code will have a negative impact on your energy systems and health. If at any time you find that you have transgressed your code, look at the reasons why, resolve to never do this again and forgive yourself. Use your failure as a step towards wisdom.

Life, the teacher, will present you with many opportunities to break your moral code. Put another way, you have ample chances to 'walk your talk'. In some instances, you may have to exert fortitude to live up to it. A weak character and a lack of ethics usually go hand in hand.

The Times News Service of London ran an article in 2005 about a survey that found that one in four British students admitted to copying and pasting material from the internet and then presenting it as their own. One in five said that they regard plagiarism as an acceptable practice. The article, to my mind, confirms what I have been saying about moral justification!

There is no moral precept that does not have something inconvenient about it.
— Denis Diderot

Truthfulness involves the ability to be honest about our failings. We may hide our faults from others but should never hide them from ourselves. Hiding our failings or trying to make excuses for our behaviour will not be of benefit to us.

To me the highest thing, after God, is my honour.
— Ludwig van Beethoven, composer

An honest man is the noblest work of God. — Alexander Pope

Shakespeare in his wisdom said, "This above all: to thine own self be true".

All the great religions talk about a code of honour.

It is easier to fight for one's principles than to live up to them.
— Alfred Adler

CREATING YOUR OWN REALITY

What is this term *'creating your own reality'*? We hear it so often but do you really know what it means? You will once you finish reading this section.

How?

Creating your own reality is really creating your own happiness and experiences by being able to direct your life along a chosen path. Creating your own reality comes from a mind-set – whether it is positive or negative – that what you put out to the universe, is what you will manifest.

Creating your own reality and self-worth

You will not be able to create your own reality if you are unable to accept gifts from others. We have spoken about not having the self-worth to be able to receive from others elsewhere in this workbook. The Universe will not give you large gifts of abundance, if you can't receive small gifts of abundance.

STOP
Are you enslaved by your own opinions
and beliefs about yourself?

Journal: ....
....
....
....

Snapshot – *Creating my own reality*

*I was about twenty-seven and had been a builder all my working life. I started off as an apprentice bricklayer. To start with I loved it - there was a freedom in working and earning my own living. I have always been an outdoor person and so with the sun on my back and the blue sky above, it was great. But after a time there was a little voice in me that said, '**Is this all there is? Can I not do something else?**' The outer voice said, '**Who are you kidding, what could you do? Besides you can't write or spell and you don't know anything about anything other than putting one brick on top of another. Create your own reality ha, what a joke**'.*
Luckily I listened to that first voice and I ignored my so-called station in life. I overlooked the inadequacies in my abilities. I knew that somehow it would all turn out OK and so I ask you to be the judge. I owned and ran a computer software company where our programmers created business software. We sold to many countries throughout the world and had a large user base. In the end I empowered my staff to take over the company and moved out to focus on writing and teaching. If, when I was a bricklayer, I had taken the advice of that outer voice, by now I would have a bad back, skin cancer, and not nearly as creative a life.

If I did not listen to that inner voice, it is unlikely that I would have become a writer, as I would have been too timid. If I had stayed as a builder I would have been fine but look at what I would have missed out on! What potential can I still aspire to because I listened to that inner voice? I loved my company and making it grow, I enjoyed the creativity of getting an idea for a software programme, researching it, creating it and then taking it to the market to see if it was going to be a winner or a flop. I love my writing and the fact that it helps people to a better life. I have become a teacher, a teacher of wisdom and lessons in life – have you any idea how wonderful it is to be able to help people like this? If I had not listened to that inner voice, my intuition, that told me I could be something better, it is unlikely that I would be in this situation. This book would not have been written, nor my other work. I get emails and telephone calls from people thanking me for helping them through something that I have written. I am truly blessed, because I listened. I have created my own reality.

You create your own reality by every thought you have, by your focus, your faith. You can only create your own reality when you know who you are and are happy with that person.

Certainly, I believe it is possible to be able to create our own reality. But there is much work that is required first. The following ten rules need to be applied.

1) you must have **no anxiety** within your mind; it must be balanced and clear, without fear or guilt.

2) is that **there must not be any negativity** within you, otherwise you push that which you want away.

3) is to **trust** that what you desire will happen (elsewhere in the workbook there is a section on trust).

4), without **vision** it will not emerge; you must be able to see it CLEARLY before it comes.

5) requirement is that you have to **believe it is already here** and not to come in the future, otherwise it will always be in the future.

6), be proactive, because without **effort** on you part it will not come to you. In action there is hope; in action vibrations are created.

7) is to **let go**, as if you want something too much you can chase it away. This may seem like a contradiction on the fourth rule about visualising, but it isn't. This is because you only visualise once per day and for a few minutes. Then you let it go and remain positive, with belief and trust.

8) requirement is to believe that you are **lucky**, because to create your own life entails the coming together of many external forces in a seemingly lucky way. If you think that you are unlucky, these forces will not meet as required.

9) rule is to **claim your personal power**. We can be meek or powerful, but to create the reality that you desire, you have to be powerful.

10) trust in God to support your efforts.

So creating your own reality is possible, but if any of the above rules are not followed, you will reduce the possibility. Positive thinking as taught by motivational speakers is only one of the many requirements.

It would serve you well to memorise the above ten rules!

INTROSPECTION

Introspect on the same success issues that you recorded in your journal when focussing on success as we did. Visualise them already gained.

Journal: ....
....
....
....
....

Peace

No one is likely to be able to create their own reality if they are not at peace with themselves. For any sort of abundance to flow, you have to be peaceful. An agitated mind will only create a reality of agitation. Things flow when you can let go and you can only let go when you are at peace. Peace comes from knowing that your spiritual aspect is eternal and nothing external can damage you.

LUCK

If you want fortuitous events (luck) in your life, it is up to you to create them. You create you own lucky reality by knowing, for instance, that …

Chance favours the prepared mind. — *Unknown*

Luck is the result of attitude, enthusiasm, dedication and consistency. As Gary Player, a Grand Slam winning golfer said, **"The more I practise, the luckier I get"** We attract or repel luck by the way we think. If you think you are lucky, you are more likely to be so. Remember the story about the replacing of my geyser? That is what I mean about attracting fortune. If you think you are unlucky, it will be so. Sad and habitually negative people are not lucky people.

STOP
Do you consider yourself lucky or unlucky? If so, why?

Journal: ……………………………………………………………………………………..
……………………………………………………………………………………………………
……………………………………………………………………………………………………
……………………………………………………………………………………………………
……………………………………………………………………………………………………

As we get back what we put out, if we put out negativity we get back negativity, which some people may see as bad luck. If you put out love and trust and positive thoughts, you get those back, which would seem like luck. Therefore, it is trust and faith that creates good luck and fear and distrust that creates bad luck. So although the word is called 'luck', it is really attitude.

Gratitude supports luck!

Now is the time (living the present moment)

Outside my window, a new day I see, only I can determine what kind of day it will be.
It can be busy and sunny, laughing and gay, or boring and cold, unhappy and grey.
My state of mind is the determining key, for I am the person I let myself be.

- Unknown

In managing yourself, there is only one time that ever existed and that time is right now.

> **STOP**
> **How often can you say you are truly in the present moment?**
> **At any stage today have you noticed the beauty**
> **that surrounds you? Stop reading, pause**
> **and take note of your surroundings. Go on do it.**
> **Acknowledge how good it is and then continue reading.**
> **When you paused, could you detect a feeling?**
> **Were you impatient, relaxed, happy, discontented?**
> **To know yourself, you have to**
> **take the time to feel what is going on in your head.**

Journal: ....
....
....
....
....

The Past and the Future

Was the past any better than what you have at present? We put down anchors into the past which keep us there. Perhaps you think the memories of yesterday seem sweeter than your current circumstances. Those times may have been great but if you are continually living in the past, you are not giving the present a chance. Some people may not have sweet memories, but may still be perpetuating disaster because of being stuck in the past – self-fulfilling prophecies of doom.

When we mourn the past, we do so from two perspectives. We may be 'crying over spilt milk'. <u>Don't let yesterday's spilt milk curdle today's cream</u>. Clean it up! The second attachment to the past is regret, which is usually associated with loss: lost love, a job, or even youth. Time does heal, if we allow it. Remember, when your energy is consumed in the past, you cannot manifest for the future. To achieve a brighter future, you have to let go of the past.

Take note - while you are manifesting in the present for a rosier future, do not forget to live your life to the full in the now. In the future you will still have your day-to-day realities - carrying out the garbage, picking up the dog poo and there will still be lessons to learn. An obsession with the future can create dissatisfaction with the present.

For now focus on the good and appreciate what you have. By expressing gratitude, you create a positive platform from which you generate your new life in the future.

In reality, your past and future do not exist. Your past is only a memory and your future is still in the creation process in your mind. The only thing you have that is tangible is the here and now. Living In the present moment is all there is.

You only create a bright future from a sunny now.

STOP
Where does your mind live most of the time,
in the past, present or in the future?
Is there a subject that takes up an excessive amount of your
thought processes, either in the past, or in the future?

Journal: ....
....
....
....
....

How often have you argued with a partner or loved one, when it seemed senseless? There is a good chance that at the time, either you or the other person was not centred. After the hostilities, with reflection it is likely to show that the disagreement was invariably the result of built-up resentment or anger from the past. For this to happen, clearly you or the other party could not have been in the present moment. It was not that you didn't love your partner. It was the result of an aggravation derived from something that happened yesterday that you allowed to run wild in your head. When you are in the present moment and focused, senseless arguments such as these no longer occur.

Some people feel the rain: others just get wet. — Roger Miller

> **STOP**
> **Where do your fears lie? Are they a result of the past?**
> **Are they about something which might happen in the future?**

Journal: ....
....
....
....

We all have responsibilities. They arise each day. We can handle each day's responsibilities as they come. But when we add tomorrow's responsibility and yesterday's anguish onto today's then we become over burdened.

Dost thou love life? Then do not squander time; for that's the stuff life is made of.

— Benjamin Franklin

One Task at a Time

You can only do one task at a time, so train your mind to concentrate on only one thing at a time.

Over the years, I have learned that when I remain in the present moment and concentrate on one chore at a time, I am less tired at the end of the day than when my mind is a kaleidoscope of thoughts. When I allow my mind to focus on doing this or that, rush, hurry or panic, it wears me out as I am sure it wears you out too. It is not necessarily the long hours and the work load that exhaust us, it is the stress we bring to it, the self-imposed pressure. Do not do the next job in your mind whilst working on the current job – stay present even with the most mundane job.

No tomorrow

Just for today, all of today, pretend that there is no tomorrow or any other day. As you go through this day, you may think, 'Oh, tomorrow I have to do…' Pass it from your mind. To remind you to do this, tie a piece of string around your wrist. If you start to set goals for the future, pass them from your mind, as there is no tomorrow.

As you drive, you may contemplate buying a new car: pass it from your mind. Or you may think that it would be nice to have an overseas holiday: pass it from your mind and so on.

Doing this is very liberating. Try it and you will see what I mean, but more importantly it will show you how often you live in the past or the future and not for today. It is hard to enjoy the present moment when you are living in the future.

> **STOP**
> **Tie that piece of string around your wrist and only live in today. As you go through the day record how often you caught yourself living either in the future of the past.**

Record these: ....
....
....
....
....

STRESS

A little stress is not necessarily a bad thing. For instance, I'll bet that the butterflies Roger Bannister felt at the start of his final attempt to break the four-minute mile helped propel him just that much faster. It is when stress is out of control or entrenched, that it becomes detrimental. When we live stressfully, it becomes internalised and starts to have debilitating effects.

Some symptoms of stress are tiredness, irritability bordering on anger, lack of appetite and reduced sexual performance. There are many more. In your search to know yourself and also understand stress, you need to see if you have any of these symptoms. If you do, they will usually be represented by a feeling in your body. You need to know what this feeling is and what causes it. To know what it feels like, you need to be in the present moment and focus on it. Get to know the feeling. By doing so, the next time it occurs, you can focus on it and it will reduce. Once you know the reasons for your feeling, you can adopt methods to reduce and eliminate it.

If you solve your recurring problems, as discussed throughout this book - manage to overcome your 'broke syndrome', improve self-esteem issues, or if you can control your life instead of it controlling you; when your relationships work and you are able to stick to a job which you enjoy, when you eliminate fear and guilt from your life and are more self-reliant; if you have a moral code that you live up to and you reduce your anger and find it easier to control your emotions; if you know that there is a purpose to life - then you are less likely to carry stress. When you become successful and overcome your failure belief, as your confidence grows and you develop a positive attitude, as you stop complaining about life or people and when you can love and be loved, your stress levels will decrease.

Funny, all those things that reduce or eliminate stress are the very same topics that this book teaches!

Stress and Worry

Sometimes there is a real reason to worry. Mostly, the perceived reasons for worry are unfounded.
If you have trust, there is no need for worry.

Are you a worrier? ....
....
....
....

Some people are perpetual worriers. You need to make sure that if you are a worrier, you must STOP, other wise you are an obvious candidate for stress-related illnesses. Habitual 'worriers' are stuck in a most debilitating and negative mode of behaviour. To find out whether you are a worrier (once again) you have to know yourself. Ask people who are close to you to give you their opinions. Search your feelings and attitudes, monitor your anxieties and feelings. If you don't, then you will roll through the years until you are prematurely rolled into your coffin.
The definition of a worrier is a person whose mind churns out concerns, i.e., their thoughts are allowed to run wild.

INTROSPECTION

Go into introspection for about ten minutes and search your mind for signs of worry. Record the results.

Journal: ....
....
....
....
....

Worry and Manifestation

Do you realise that by worrying about something you are likely to perpetuate the very thing that you want to avoid? When we focus on something, which is what we do when we worry, we give it energy. What we focus on is what we manifest.

We are not born worriers. We develop anxiety over time. Worrying is a habit and like any habit can be broken. Nothing in the world stays the same. Things either get better or worse. Nothing will improve until something intervenes. So apply change to those aspects of your life that cause anxiety.

Treat all disasters as if they were trivialities but never treat a triviality as if it were a disaster. — Quentin Crisp

Stress and Your Work

Do you find meaning in your work? If not, why not? If not, it is your own doing. Look for meaning or quit and do something else. As you spend about a third of your life at work, it makes sense to enjoy it.

Remember what you learned under the topic earlier on CHANGE? Change is good and leads to growth. Don't be afraid to change your position. Years ago I read that 75% of the top CEO's of Fortune 500 companies had changed their job consistently every two years or thereabouts, prior to becoming the CEO of those companies! In their case constant change took them upwards.

If you work hard, but love what you do, you are less likely to be stressed than if you don't like it. Enthusiasm is nine-tenths of the way to success.

The highest reward for a person's work is not what they get for it, but what they become by it.
— Unknown

Creation is a better means of self-expression than possession; it is through creating, not possessing, that life is revealed.
— Unknown

PATIENCE = Faith and reduced stress

We must be more like trees; when they have snow on their branches, they just wait until the snow melts. When there is a drought, they wait until the rains come. If there are floods, trees just wait until the water recedes.

Trees, do not 'try' to grow, they just grow. Trees do not hunger for spring when it is winter, nor do they want autumn, when it is summer. They just allow the natural flow of things to happen, one day at a time, one week at time, one month at a time.

Whoever said **patience is a virtue** knew what they were talking about.

STOP
**Think for a minute about how impatient
you get when you are caught in traffic or in queues.
Now think about how it stresses you.**

Journal: ……………………………………………………………………………………………
……………………………………………………………………………………………
……………………………………………………………………………………………
……………………………………………………………………………………………
……………………………………………………………………………………………

"Infinite patience produces immediate results"
- A Course in Miracles

All your hard work to find yourself will only come to you if you work on yourself with patience. Your desires are like the tide, which gradually flows in and slowly recedes. You do not get high tide one minute and low tide the next. It is a process and so is your connecting with your inner self.

STOP
Do you consider yourself patient or impatient?

Journal……………………………………………………………………………………………
……………………………………………………………………………………………
……………………………………………………………………………………………

....
....

Impatience creates stress

It is fine to want to get ahead but don't get impatient. I have seen it in so many people. People feel they 'should' be further down the road than they are, whether in business or with the accumulation of material possessions. By doing so they put undue pressure on themselves. They stress and panic that they 'should' be working harder. By doing so, they create dissatisfaction with their current state of affairs, which only serves to block their growth even further.

Being impatient to the point of becoming stressed will lead to ill health. Stop it, before it stops you.

FREEDOM

"Freedom's just another word for nothing left to lose" (as sung by Janice Joplin, music and lyrics by Kris Kristofferson) and is a great way to start this section about Freedom.

Most people are not free in the real sense of the word. We may be able to come and go as we please but we have constraints that inhibit our real freedom. These constraints are mostly self-imposed and mental. They are imposed both by our need to conform to what society dictates as a result of the limitations we place upon ourselves.

To give you an example, imagine two people living together. They love each other but fight like crazy. It would seem that they just cannot get along. Remaining in this environment reduces their freedom of expression. He is not free to stay and enjoy the fruits of his love, nor is he free to move out. She is restricted by the frustration. They are, in effect, stuck. Both parties are imposing their own limitations.

Given below are topics on freedom which all come from this book. You will see that without knowing yourself you can not have real freedom.

Freedom and Death
If you are abnormally worried about death, you will be killing your freedom while living.

Freedom and Ego

If you have read the section on ego, you will realise that we place clamps upon ourselves by trying to impress our peers with our hair do's, the clothes we wear, the cars we drive – these are limiting.

Freedom and Work

If you are not happy with the work you do, or the company you work for, you reduce your freedom.

Freedom and Attachments

Attachments limit your freedom. As your remove them, you will experience the joy of greater control over your life. Release attachments and gain freedom: after all, there is freedom in simplicity.

Freedom and Stress

Stress kills freedom stone dead. A lack of freedom can create stress. Remember *'In action there is hope and freedom'*.

STOP
What does it take for you to be free every minute of every day? There are moments in your Life when you have freedom, but these are likely to be few as you are probably tied up in knots carrying and holding on to the drama of life.

Introspection on these: ....
....
....
....
....

Freedom and Trust

By trusting that your life has a purpose, you create the freedom to allow yourself to achieve that purpose.

Freedom and a Moral Code
A moral code will offer greater freedom.

Freedom and Money
Without money to pay the rent or buy food, you impose limitations on aspects of your lives. Money helps to buy freedom. It helps to purchase your way out of limitation. Money helps you to gain free time. Notice in the above, I say money 'helps'. Money on its own will not give you freedom, as the freedom or lack thereof is self-imposed by your mind-set. Yet a lack of money will curtail your freedom.

Even if you have lots of money, the fear of losing can it block your freedom.

Freedom and Forgiveness
When you do not forgive a person or situation you create mental bondage. Once you have forgiven, a weight is removed.

Freedom and Emotions
Your guilt, sadness and worries will all reduce your effectiveness. You will not have the freedom of creativity or feel the joy of going forward.

Freedom and the Thought Process
Negativity reduces freedom. Positive thoughts help to expand your freedom.

Freedom and Self- Worth
All lack of self-worth contributes to a life of "virtual imprisonment".

Freedom and Confidence
Without confidence in yourself, there will be many unachieved goals in your life. Your lack of confidence reduces your freedom to expand yourself. It will kill your creativity.

Freedom and Quietness
You learn what freedom of the mind is when you learn to become quiet, to still the mind.

Nothing can bring you peace but yourself.
– Ralph Waldo Emerson

I began this topic with **"Freedom's just another word for nothing left to lose"** as sung by Janice Joplin. Janice would have known this better than most, as she was a slave to drugs. Mental freedom, in the real sense of the word, evaded her. In the end the drugs killed her!

To summarise, know that your freedom, or lack of, is self-imposed as a direct result of what you perceive and think about life. When you remove the self-imposed constraints you create a freedom that allows you to grow, to be happy.

INTROSPECTION

Consider all the above sections on freedom. What are your limitations and how can you remove imposed limitations on freedom?

Journal……………………………………………………………………………………..
……………………………………………………………………………………………..
……………………………………………………………………………………………..
……………………………………………………………………………………………..
……………………………………………………………………………………………..

AT THE END OF YOUR LIFE

Over the years I have asked many old people to tell me about the things they regret. Most of them are not overly concerned with their bad choices or things they considered to be failures. Their regret was more for the things <u>that they did not do!</u>

INTROSPECTION

Once in your familiar and safe alpha state, pretend that you are at the end of your life. Consider the things that you might regret not having done, such as:

- Gaining knowledge

- Loving humanity more
- Travelling to exotic places
- Finding a fulfilling hobby
- Focusing on health issues
- Gaining wealth
- Finding Happiness
- Practising your spirituality

The list is endless.

Journal: ....
....
....
....
....

NOW THAT YOU KNOW YOURSELF, GO OUT AND LIVE EACH DAY AS IF IT WAS YOUR FIRST.

What is the first thing that you are going to do? ....
....
....

And the second? ....
....
....
....

And the third? ....
....
....
....

And the fourth? ....
....
....
....

> **STOP**
> Have you lived 10,000 days,
> or have you lived the same day 10,000 times?
> - Unknown

END NOTES

Putting this book together has been a work of love, dedication and education. I mentioned at the start of the book that we teach what we most need to learn. This book has taken me many years to write. I have had, and still do have, lots to learn. Many of the lessons I teach I have had to learn and in some cases re-learn many times.

As a teacher, I also have to live these concepts. The challenge is no easier for me than it is for you. I still make mistakes, get angry and resentful. Sometimes I am slow to forgive. Being human means that on occasions I forget who I am and will lose sight of my connectedness to The Universe. But nowadays, I react faster and reduce the effects by re-aligning myself to the 'light' that Source offers. I do not languish for months, obsessed with the baggage that I pick up along the way. I know that I must always be alert to the 'old issues' that rear their ugly heads.

It is now easier to be at one with the greatness that lies within me, as it is to recognise the greatness within my fellow human beings, a greatness that had always been there, yet I had previously failed to see.

The understanding of the way of The Universe that, 'What you put out is what you get back' is also a wonderful source of inspiration. My aim is to incorporate this knowledge so that it becomes an intrinsic part of who I am, to become it, to internalise it, experience it and to turn it into consciousness.

The book began by stating that until you understand and clear some of your earth issues, you are unlikely to achieve the spiritual growth that is your right. As I remove each issue, my understanding of the way of The Universe increases. When my mind is not preoccupied with my human problems, I see and know God. I allow myself to be open to the Intelligence, to receive its wisdom and to continue growing towards the light and away from the darkness.

Now that you have read the book, you know Pat Grayson. You understand a person who has made many mistakes in his life. You also know about my growth. For me to inspire you, to improve your life, I have been as authentic and transparent as possible, exposing my deepest fears. If you derive one benefit from this work then my exposure will have been worth it.

Understanding yourself and The Divine that resides within you is a voyage of self-discovery. You learn that the journey never ends. By learning, you create a sense of who you are, which allows you to navigate more smoothly, faster and less perilously across the ocean of your life. By looking within you will discover uncharted emotions and thoughts. You will find yourself venturing into what was once forbidden territory. You will return with the treasure of understanding. This voyage is not likely to be a smooth advancement. It will happen in fits and starts.

But it's not Pat Grayson that you need to learn about, it's you. I have only been along for the ride for the purpose of being an example and perhaps a guide.

Hopefully, you now know more about yourself than you did before you started the book. I trust that you will continue to use the work-book, as each time you work through it you will have further growth and improvement.

There is a Chinese proverb that says; "**I dreamed a thousand new paths.... I woke and walked the old one**". Please don't do that. Find a better path, your true path.

There is a simple truth - find yourself and you find love. It is my sincere hope that this book has taken you towards achieving both.

Pat Grayson

INTROSPECTIONS – IN GREATER DETAIL

TOPIC ONE – FEAR

Fear is your greatest enemy if you let it dominate you. If you introspect on it, it will melt. Apply the methods given above. When you are in deep relaxation, bring to your mind a fear that plagues you. Give total focus to it. Have no anger or aggression. Bring in a resource to overcome fear, such as courage and confidence. See yourself behaving with these new resources. Direct joy at it and watch it disappear.

Typical fears that we have:

- Fear of a lack of money
- Fear of ridicule (afraid to branch out on our own)
- Fear of bad health, becoming incapacitated
- Fear of a lack of love
- Fear of old age and death

Once you know that it works, you can apply the focus any time of the day.

Introspection journal notes: ....

....

....

....

....

....

....

....

....

TOPIC TWO - THINGS I RESENT

- People with money
- Poor people
- People from a different race or colour
- Educated people
- Uneducated people
- Aggressive people
- Nondescript people

I suggest that you first identify your prejudices and record them so you can do some thought-provoking work on them. Do they serve you and is it correct to 'label' all the people you place in those boxes as being bad or wrong? Record your prejudices so you can work on them over a period of months.

What is it that you resent? ....

....

....

....

....

....

....

....

....

TOPIC THREE - THINGS I FEEL I SHOULD DO, OTHERWISE I FEEL GUILTY

Look at the things that you feel guilty about. When we apply the word 'should', it is usually associated with 'a guilt trip' we lay on ourselves. Below is a sample list. Make your own and realise that you 'could' do them if you choose.

Some people feel guilty if they think they:

- Should work harder
- Should spend less money
- Should earn more money
- Should go on a diet
- Should visit someone
- Should have cleaned the house

Make your own 'should' list and replace 'should' with 'could' then decide which you could do if you chose to.

When do you feel guilty? ....

....

....

....

....

....

....

TOPIC FOUR - YOUR FAILURE SYNDROME

Do you have a failure syndrome?

Perhaps your 'failure syndrome' is a script that was written when you were a child. Whatever your 'failure syndrome' is, write it down as you should know it by now.

No experience is wasted and what you consider to be failures are merely lessons in life.

INTROSPECTION

Make a list of your so-called failures and go into introspection. Experience each one separately and dissipate it. Run the movie and see each experience as you would have wanted it to be, creating a more favourable outcome. Towards the end of your reflection time introduce the thought, 'I am successful'.

A Sample List of 'Failures' that could set you up for a failure syndrome:

- Failure at school
- Not being athletic in school
- Not being one of the popular girls or guys
- Flunking out of university
- Divorce
- Never marrying
- Going bankrupt
- Not having children

What is your failure syndrome? ....

....
....
....
....
....
....
....
....
....
....

TOPIC FIVE - YOUR MISSION STATEMENT FOR A WORKABLE LIFE

Do you have a mission statement for life? If not, why not?

Mine is and has been for several years 'To empower myself, so that I can empower others'. This book is testimony to my striving to fulfil my mission statement.

How can you achieve your ambitions in life if you do not know what you want to achieve? A mission statement gives you a set direction. When you have a mission statement based on those things that are important to you, you are more likely to become what the mission statement suggests.

A mission statement for life is a wonderful topic to introspect on. Go within and identify what is important to you in life. Don't stop there. Look for reasons why these things are important to you.

Document your mission statement. Don't be afraid to spend lots of time on it, as a good mission statement is a lighthouse for you in the stormy seas of life.

The things that you could look at are:

- Family
- Morals
- Work and business
- Leisure time
- Goals
- Exercise and health

Write your mission statements: ....
....
....
....
....
....
....
....
....
....

TOPIC SIX – DEATH

Many people fear death. To understand your death issues, I suggest a meditation on dying. Go into your introspection and see yourself on your deathbed, where death is only a day or two away.

Introspect on:

- Are you afraid of the actual dying or the sickness and pain that may be the cause of your dying?
- Does it grieve you to think that you will not be here any longer or that life will continue without you?
- What about Judgement Day types of issues? Are you concerned that there could be a fire and brimstone party waiting for you?
- If you were to die right now, would you feel complete? Would there be regrets or remorse? Would you feel that your life had been worth it? Should there have been more accomplishments to give it value?
- Would there be unfinished business, such as: anger, need for revenge, a sour or unfinished relationship?
- What about spiritual matters? Would you feel comfortable with your current beliefs and actions?

You may find that the issues you discover on your death introspection have a governing affect on your life.

It is likely that when you are comfortable with your death issues you will be more comfortable in life.

Journalise what you learnt from the introspection………………………………………………..

………………………………………………………………………………………………………..
………………………………………………………………………………………………………..
………………………………………………………………………………………………………..
………………………………………………………………………………………………………..
………………………………………………………………………………………………………..
………………………………………………………………………………………………………..
………………………………………………………………………………………………………..
………………………………………………………………………………………………………..

TOPIC SEVEN – A REVIEW OF YOUR LIFE

As you have embarked on the worthy cause of knowing yourself, here is an introspection, or rather several introspections that will help you in knowing who you are and the emotions that have created you.

Do an introspection for each ten years of your life thus far. That is, each session covers a ten-year period. The first session would be from your earliest memories up until the age of ten. The next session would be from ages ten to twenty and so on. Only do one period per day, and do them on consecutive days.

As you do each period, try to remember all the major events. Feel the emotions around those events. At the end of each introspection record the findings in your journal.
When you have done your last review introspection, re-work each ten year period in your journal to see links and patterns over the years. These review introspections are very powerful. You will be stunned at the things you will learn about yourself.

The review: ....

....

....

....

....

....

....

....

....

....

....

....

....

....

....

....

....

....

TOPIC EIGHT - TELL ME ABOUT YOUR PARENTS

It is for good reasons that psychologists ask this question when they receive a new patient. You parents and their behaviour has partially formed your personality and thought structures. Therefore it is a good idea to be aware of the influence that your parents had on you. And the best way to understand that influence is to do introspections on both parents and incidents that you experienced with them.

About your parents: ....

....

....

....

....
....
....
....
....

Contemplation is responsible daydreaming

TOPIC NINE – WRITING ABOUT YOUR ISSUES

Another good clearing method is to write about your issues. By writing about these, you are forced to focus on them. This will open you up to rich understanding, which normally lies hidden in the subconscious. Writing about my own issues is how this book came about!

Writing is a wonderful way to clarify your understanding. When you can verbalise an issue, it goes from being a jumbled concept in your mind to one of clarity. Writing brings all the components together so you can identify the emotional issues.

When you write about painful experiences, you open yourself up to clearing those issues. It is cathartic and insightful. Allow yourself to let go.

The writings become records. Records of your past can be testimonials to your progress.

YOUR JOURNAL

Now that you have finished Know ThySelf, I suggest that you spend the next few weeks going over all that you have written in your journal.

When ready, start the workbook again as each time you work through it, you will gain more understanding of who you are and what life really means to you.

For information on Graysonian Press and its range of inspirational books.
www.graysonian.com pat@graysonian.com

0450260348 Australia - **+ 27 11 4311274** South Africa

About the author

Pat is an Australian, an entrepreneur, a writer, a publisher and a teacher of metaphysical and human issues. He is fifty-eight.

Other works by Pat Grayson

What would you do if you knew you could not fail?

How to Write – Right!

Yogi, the tails and teachings of a suburban alpha doggy

Calling You Will (published by John Hunt Books)

Workshops

Pat conducts workshops and undertakes public speaking, where he addresses both individuals and groups in private or corporate settings. All his presentations are based on his writings.

Know ThySelf, a twenty-session course, is based on the workbook.

How to Write – Right!

What would you do if you knew you could not fail? Positivity workshops. These are for companies and private groups.

If you have any suggestions on how to improve this workbook, I would love to hear from you.

REFERENCE

A Course in Miracles
A Pilgrims in Aquarius – David Spangler
A Little Light on Spiritual Laws – Diana Cooper
Anatomy of Spirit – Caroline Myss (Ph.D)
As I see It – Author A Friedman
Ask You Angles – Alma Parker, Timothy Wyllie, Andrew Rame
Awareness – Anthony De Mello
Balado
Beyond Birth and Death – AC Bhaktivedanta Swami Prabhupada
Bhagavad-Gita, As it is - AC Bhaktivedanta Swami Prabhupada
Classical Greek, CM Bowra
Collins English Dictionary
Collins Gem English Dictionary
Conversations with God – Neale Donald Walsh
Get Smart, Get Rich – John Laurens
Grow Rich While you Sleep – Ben Sweetland
Hatha Yoga – Yogi Ramacharaka
Lamps of Lights – Eichler Watson
Mahatma Gandhi – BR Nanda
Mans Search for Meaning – Victor Frankel
Meditation and the Mind of Man – Hurbert Puryear, Mark Thurston
Mother Theresa, Her Life, Her Work, Her Message – Jose Luis Gonzalez
Script Analysis – Eric Berne
Seven Miracles of Management – Alan Downs
The Celestine Prophecy – James Redfield
The Concise Oxford Dictionary
The Everyman's Dictionary of Religion and Philosophy by Geddes Macgregor
The Hidden Messages in Water – Masaru Emoto
The Hutchinson Concise Encyclopaedia
The Invitation – Oriah Mountain Dreamer
The Master Key to Riches – Napoloeon Hill
The Mystics of Islam – Reymond a Nickolson
The New King James Bible, New Testament, 1997 (Gideon's)
The Path – The School of Truth
The Power of Positive thinking – Norman Vincent Peale
The Re-Enchantment of Every Day Life – Thomas Moore
The Seven Habits of Highly Effective People - Stephen Covey
The Teachings of Buddha – B Kyokai
The Twelve Gateways to Human Potential – Dan Millman
Thinking Big – Earnie J Zelinski
You can Heal Your Life – Louise Hay
Your Erroneous Zones – Dr Wayne Dyer
Why People Don't heal and How They Can – Caroline Myss (Ph.D)

www.ingramcontent.com/pod-product-compliance
Lightning Source LLC
Chambersburg PA
CBHW051148290426
44108CB00019B/2651